THE COMPLETE
NINJA DUAL ZONE
AIR FRYER
COOKBOOK UK 2024

**1800 Days of Effortless, Delicious Recipes
for Beginners Using British Ingredients**

Mary Waters

CONTENTS

Fish And Seafood Recipes

Sandwiches And Burgers Recipes

Appetizers And Snacks

INTRODUCTION

✽ ✽ ✽ The Complete Ninja Dual Zone Air Fryer Cookbook UK 2024: 1800 Days of Effortless, Delicious Recipes for Beginners Using British Ingredients ✽ ✽ ✽

Are you ready to revolutionize your cooking with the Ninja Dual Zone Air Fryer? Look no further! This comprehensive cookbook is your ultimate guide to mastering effortless, healthy, and mouthwatering meals using British ingredients.

What makes this cookbook a must-have for your kitchen:

☑ 1800 Days of Varied Recipes: From quick breakfasts to gourmet dinners, never run out of ideas!

☑ Beginner-Friendly: Step-by-step instructions and tips make air frying accessible to everyone.

☑ UK-Centric: All recipes use easily available British ingredients and UK measurements.

☑ Dual Zone Mastery: Learn to cook two different dishes simultaneously, saving time and energy.

☑ Health-Conscious: Enjoy crispy, delicious meals with up to 75% less fat than traditional frying.

Discover a world of culinary delights, including:

🔍 Breakfast recipes

🥘 Vegetables recipes

🐟 Fish and seafood recipes

🥩 Pork recipes

🥩 Beef recipes

🍗 Poultry recipes

🍤 Snack and dessert recipes

And so much more...

Whether you're a busy professional, a health-conscious foodie, or a culinary novice, this cookbook will transform your Ninja Dual Zone Air Fryer into your most valuable kitchen ally.

Don't miss out on this opportunity to elevate your cooking game! Click "Buy Now" and embark on a journey of flavour, health, and culinary excellence with your Ninja Dual Zone Air Fryer!

Bread And Breakfast

Easy Corn Dog Cupcakes

Servings: 6 | Prep Time: 10 Minutes | Cooking Time: 30 Minutes

Ingredients:

- 1 cup cornbread mix
- 2 teaspoons granulated sugar
- Salt to taste
- 180 g cream cheese
- 3 tablespoons butter, melted
- 1 egg
- ¼ cup minced onions
- 1 teaspoon dried parsley
- 2 beef hot dogs, sliced and cut into half-moons

Directions:

1. Preheat air fryer at 180°C/350°F.
2. Combine cornbread, sugar, and salt in a bowl.
3. In another bowl, whisk cream cheese, parsley, butter, and egg.
4. Pour wet ingredients to dry ingredients and toss to combine. Fold in onion and hot dog pieces.
5. Transfer it into 8 greased silicone cupcake liners. Place it in the frying basket and Bake for 8-10 minutes.
6. Serve right away.

Variations & Ingredients Tips:

- Use different types of sausage, such as Italian or chorizo, for a variety of flavors.
- Add some shredded cheddar cheese or jalapeños to the batter for extra flavor and heat.
- Serve the corn dog cupcakes with a side of ketchup or mustard for dipping.

Per Serving: Calories: 290; Total Fat: 22g; Saturated Fat: 11g; Cholesterol: 80mg; Sodium: 520mg; Total Carbs: 18g; Fiber: 1g; Sugars: 5g; Protein: 7g

Orange Trail Oatmeal

Servings: 4 | Prep Time: 15 Minutes | Cooking Time: 20 Minutes

Ingredients:

- 1 1/2 cups quick-cooking oats
- 1/3 cup light brown sugar
- 1 egg
- 1 tsp orange zest
- 1 tbsp orange juice
- 2 tbsp whole milk
- 2 tbsp honey
- 2 tbsp butter, melt-
- ed
- 2 tsp dried cranberries
- 1 tsp dried blueberries
- 1/8 tsp ground nutmeg
- Salt to taste
- 1/4 cup pecan pieces

Directions:

1. Preheat air fryer at 165°C/325°F.
2. Combine all ingredients in a bowl.
3. Press mixture into a greased cake pan.
4. Place pan in air fryer basket and roast for 8 minutes.
5. Let cool for 5 minutes before slicing and serving.

Variations & Ingredients Tips:

- Use old-fashioned oats for a heartier texture.
- Substitute maple syrup for the honey.
- Top with fresh berries and yogurt.

Per Serving: Calories: 305; Total Fat: 12g; Saturated Fat: 4g; Cholesterol: 50mg; Sodium: 75mg; Total Carbs: 45g; Dietary Fiber: 4g; Sugars: 23g; Protein: 6g

Farmers Market Quiche

Servings: 4 | Prep Time: 15 Minutes | Cooking Time: 35 Minutes

Ingredients:

- 4 button mush-rooms
- ¼ medium red bell pepper
- 1 teaspoon ex-tra-virgin olive oil
- One 23 cm pie crust, at room tem-perature
- ¼ cup grated carrot
- ¼ cup chopped, fresh baby spinach leaves
- 3 eggs, whisked
- 59 ml half-and-half
- ½ teaspoon thyme
- ½ teaspoon sea salt
- 57 g crumbled goat cheese or feta

Directions:

1. In a medium bowl, toss the mushrooms and bell pepper with extra-virgin olive oil; place into the air fryer basket. Set the temperature to 200°C/400°F for 8 minutes, stirring after 4 min-utes. Remove from the air fryer, and roughly chop the mushrooms and bell peppers. Wipe the air fryer clean.
2. Prep an 18 cm oven-safe baking dish by spray-ing the bottom of the pan with cooking spray.
3. Place the pie crust into the baking dish; fold over and crimp the edges or use a fork to press to give the edges some shape.
4. In a medium bowl, mix together the mush-rooms, bell peppers, carrots, spinach, and eggs. Stir in the half-and-half, thyme, and salt.
5. Pour the quiche mixture into the base of the pie shell. Top with crumbled cheese.
6. Place the quiche into the air fryer basket. Set the temperature to 165°C/325°F for 30 minutes.
7. When complete, turn the quiche halfway and cook an additional 5 minutes. Allow the quiche to rest 20 minutes prior to slicing and serving.

Variations & Ingredients Tips:

- Use asparagus, zucchini or broccoli instead of mushrooms and peppers.
- Add some cooked bacon, ham or sausage for a meaty version.
- Sprinkle with chopped fresh herbs like parsley or chives before serving.

Per Serving: Calories: 315; Total Fat: 21g; Sat-urated Fat: 9g; Cholesterol: 158mg; Sodium: 517mg; Total Carbs: 21g; Dietary Fiber: 1g; Total

Sugars: 3g; Protein: 11g

Buttermilk Biscuits

Servings: 4 | Prep Time: 10 Minutes | Cooking Time: 9 Minutes

Ingredients:

- 1 cup all-purpose flour
- 1½ teaspoons bak-ing powder
- ¼ teaspoon baking soda
- ¼ teaspoon salt
- ¼ cup butter, cut into tiny cubes
- ¼ cup buttermilk, plus 2 tablespoons
- Cooking spray

Directions:

1. Preheat air fryer to 165°C/330°F.
2. In a bowl, combine flour, baking powder, soda and salt.
3. Cut in butter using knives or pastry blender un-til crumbly.
4. Stir in buttermilk until a stiff dough forms.
5. Divide dough into 4 portions and shape into biscuits.
6. Spray air fryer basket with cooking spray.
7. Place biscuits in basket and bake at 165°C/330°F for 9 minutes.

Variations & Ingredients Tips:

- Add shredded cheddar cheese or cooked bacon to the dough.
- Brush tops with melted butter before baking.
- Substitute milk and vinegar for the buttermilk if needed.

Per Serving: Calories: 230; Total Fat: 12g; Satu-rated Fat: 7g; Cholesterol: 30mg; Sodium: 460mg; Total Carbs: 25g; Dietary Fiber: 1g; Total Sugars: 1g; Protein: 4g

Seasoned Herbed Sourdough Croutons

Servings: 4 | Prep Time: 5 Minutes | Cooking Time: 7 Minutes

Ingredients:

- 4 cups cubed sourdough bread, 2.5cm cubes (about 225-g)
- 1 tablespoon olive oil
- 1 teaspoon fresh thyme leaves
- ¼ – ½ teaspoon salt
- Freshly ground black pepper

Directions:

1. Combine all ingredients in a bowl and season to taste.
2. Preheat air fryer to 205°C/400°F.
3. Toss bread cubes into air fryer and cook for 7 minutes, shaking basket 1-2 times.
4. Serve warm or store in airtight container.

Variations & Ingredients Tips:

- Use different herb combinations like rosemary, sage or Italian seasoning.
- Add parmesan cheese or garlic powder for extra flavor.
- Toss croutons with a balsamic vinaigrette after cooking.

Per Serving: Calories: 117; Total Fat: 4g; Saturated Fat: 1g; Cholesterol: 0mg; Sodium: 310mg; Total Carbs: 18g; Dietary Fiber: 1g; Total Sugars: 1g; Protein: 3g

Orange Rolls

Servings: 8 | Prep Time: 15 Minutes | Cooking Time: 10 Minutes

Ingredients:

- Parchment paper
- 85-g low-fat cream cheese
- 1 tbsp low-fat sour cream or plain yogurt
- 2 tsp sugar
- 1/4 tsp vanilla extract
- 1/4 tsp orange extract
- 1 (8 count) can organic crescent roll dough
- 1/4 cup chopped walnuts
- 1/4 cup dried cranberries
- 1/4 cup shredded sweetened coconut
- Butter-flavored cooking spray
- Orange Glaze:
- 1/2 cup powdered sugar
- 1 tbsp orange juice
- 1/4 tsp orange extract
- Dash of salt

Directions:

1. Cut parchment for air fryer basket and set aside.
2. Mix cream cheese, sour cream/yogurt, sugar, vanilla and orange extracts until smooth.
3. Preheat air fryer to 150°C/300°F.
4. Separate crescent dough into triangles. Spread cheese mix on each leaving 2.5cm border.
5. Sprinkle nuts, cranberries over cheese. Roll up from wide end.
6. Place on parchment, spray tops with cooking spray.
7. Air fry 4 rolls for 10 mins until golden.
8. Repeat with remaining rolls.
9. Make glaze and drizzle over warm rolls.

Variations & Ingredients Tips:

- Use different dried fruits or nuts.
- Substitute almond or lemon extract.
- Dust with powdered sugar instead of glaze.

Per Serving: Calories: 220; Total Fat: 12g; Saturated Fat: 4g; Cholesterol: 10mg; Sodium: 230mg; Total Carbs: 26g; Dietary Fiber: 1g; Sugars: 13g; Protein: 3g

Mini Bacon Egg Quiches

Servings: 6 | Prep Time: 10 Minutes | Cooking Time: 30 Minutes

Ingredients:

- 3 eggs
- 2 tbsp heavy cream
- 1/4 tsp Dijon mustard
- Salt and pepper to taste
- 85g cooked bacon, crumbled
- 1/4 cup grated cheddar

Directions:

1. Preheat air fryer to 175°C/350°F.
2. Beat the eggs with salt and pepper in a bowl until fluffy. Stir in heavy cream, mustard, cooked bacon, and cheese.

3. Divide the mixture between 6 greased muffin cups and place them in the frying basket.
4. Bake for 8-10 minutes.
5. Let cool slightly before serving.

Variations & Ingredients Tips:

● Use ham, sausage or smoked salmon instead of bacon.
● Add some sautéed spinach, kale or mushrooms to the mix.
● Top with sliced green onions or chopped chives.

Per Serving: Calories: 140; Total Fat: 11g; Saturated Fat: 5g; Cholesterol: 130mg; Sodium: 270mg; Total Carbs: 1g; Dietary Fiber: 0g; Total Sugars: 0g; Protein: 9g

Cheddar Cheese Biscuits

Servings: 8 | Prep Time: 15 Minutes | Cooking Time: 22 Minutes

Ingredients:

● 2⅓ cups self-rising flour
● 2 tablespoons sugar
● ½ cup (1 stick) butter, frozen for 15 minutes
● ½ cup grated Cheddar cheese, plus more to melt on top
● 1⅓ cups buttermilk
● 1 cup all-purpose flour, for shaping
● 1 tablespoon butter, melted

Directions:

1. Line a buttered 18cm metal cake pan with parchment or a silicone liner.
2. Combine self-rising flour and sugar in a bowl. Grate in frozen butter and add cheddar. Stir to coat butter and cheese with flour. Add buttermilk and stir just until no streaks of flour remain.
3. Spread all-purpose flour on a tray. Scoop 8 balls of dough into flour, coat with flour and place in prepared pan, touching each other.
4. Preheat air fryer to 193°C/380°F.
5. Transfer cake pan to air fryer basket using a foil sling. Air fry for 20 minutes, checking oc-

casionally and covering any browned parts with foil.
6. Check for doneness by inserting a toothpick into center - it should come out clean. If needed, air fry 2 more minutes.
7. Brush tops with melted butter and sprinkle more cheese if desired. Air fry 2 more minutes.
8. Remove using foil sling. Let cool briefly, then pull biscuits apart and serve immediately.

Variations & Ingredients Tips:

● Add herbs like chives, thyme or rosemary to the dough.
● Substitute milk for buttermilk, adding 1 tbsp vinegar or lemon juice.
● Brush biscuit tops with melted garlic butter.

Per Serving: Calories: 300; Total Fat: 16g; Saturated Fat: 9g; Cholesterol: 40mg; Sodium: 590mg; Total Carbs: 33g; Dietary Fiber: 1g; Total Sugars: 4g; Protein: 7g

Broccoli Cornbread

Servings: 6 | Prep Time: 10 Minutes | Cooking Time: 18 Minutes

Ingredients:

● 1 cup frozen chopped broccoli, thawed and drained
● ¼ cup cottage cheese
● 1 egg, beaten
● 2 tablespoons minced onion
● 2 tablespoons melted butter
● ½ cup all-purpose flour
● ½ cup yellow cornmeal
● 1 teaspoon baking powder
● ½ teaspoon salt
● ¼ cup milk, plus 2 tablespoons
● Cooking spray

Directions:

1. Place thawed broccoli in colander and press with a spoon to squeeze out excess moisture.
2. Stir together all ingredients in a large bowl.
3. Spray 15x15cm baking pan with cooking spray.
4. Spread batter in pan and cook at 165°C/330°F for 18 minutes or until lightly browned and

pulling away from sides.

Variations & Ingredients Tips:

- Add shredded cheddar cheese to the batter.
- Use fresh broccoli florets instead of frozen.
- Substitute greek yogurt for the cottage cheese.

Per Serving: Calories: 155; Total Fat: 6g; Saturated Fat: 3g; Cholesterol: 40mg; Sodium: 320mg; Total Carbs: 21g; Dietary Fiber: 2g; Total Sugars: 3g; Protein: 5g

- Serve with warm corn tortillas, refried beans and sliced avocado.
- Top with crumbled queso fresco or cotija cheese.
- Add some chopped jalapeños or chipotle peppers for extra heat.

Per Serving: Calories: 164; Total Fat: 11g; Saturated Fat: 3g; Cholesterol: 186mg; Sodium: 425mg; Total Carbs: 10g; Dietary Fiber: 2g; Total Sugars: 6g; Protein: 8g

Huevos Rancheros

Servings: 4 | Prep Time: 10 Minutes | Cooking Time: 45 Minutes + Cooling Time

Ingredients:

- 1 tablespoon olive oil
- 20 cherry tomatoes, halved
- 2 chopped plum tomatoes
- 59 ml tomato sauce
- 2 scallions, sliced
- 2 garlic cloves, minced
- 1 teaspoon honey
- ½ teaspoon salt
- ⅛ teaspoon cayenne pepper
- ¼ teaspoon grated nutmeg
- ¼ teaspoon paprika
- 4 eggs

Directions:

1. Preheat the air fryer to 190°C/370°F. Combine the olive oil, cherry tomatoes, plum tomatoes, tomato sauce, scallions, garlic, nutmeg, honey, salt, paprika and cayenne in an 18 cm springform pan that has been wrapped in foil to prevent leaks. Put the pan in the frying basket and Bake the mix for 15-20 minutes, stirring twice until the tomatoes are soft. Mash some of the tomatoes in the pan with a fork, then stir them into the sauce. Also, break the eggs into the sauce, then return the pan to the fryer and Bake for 2 minutes. Remove the pan from the fryer and stir the eggs into the sauce, whisking them through the sauce. Don't mix in completely. Cook for 4-8 minutes more or until the eggs are set. Let cool, then serve.

Variations & Ingredients Tips:

Morning Apple Biscuits

Servings: 6 | Prep Time: 5 Minutes | Cooking Time: 15 Minutes

Ingredients:

- 1 apple, grated
- 1 cup oat flour
- 2 tbsp honey
- 1/4 cup peanut butter
- 1/3 cup raisins
- 1/2 tsp ground cinnamon

Directions:

1. Preheat air fryer to 175°C/350°F.
2. Combine apple, flour, honey, peanut butter, raisins and cinnamon in a bowl.
3. Form into balls and flatten slightly.
4. Place on parchment paper in air fryer basket.
5. Bake for 9 minutes until lightly browned.
6. Serve warm.

Variations & Ingredients Tips:

- Use almond or cashew butter instead of peanut.
- Add chopped nuts or chocolate chips.
- Drizzle with maple syrup or dust with powdered sugar.

Per Serving: Calories: 140; Total Fat: 6g; Saturated Fat: 1g; Cholesterol: 0mg; Sodium: 45mg; 19g; Dietary Fiber: 3g; Sugars: 9g; Protein: 4g

Vegetarian Quinoa Cups

Servings: 6 | Prep Time: 10 Minutes | Cooking Time: 25 Minutes

Ingredients:

- 1 carrot, chopped
- 1 zucchini, chopped
- 4 asparagus, chopped
- ¾ cup quinoa flour
- 2 tbsp lemon juice
- ¼ cup nutritional yeast
- ¼ tsp garlic powder
- Salt and pepper to taste

Directions:

1. Preheat air fryer to 170°C/340°F.
2. Combine the vegetables, quinoa flour, water, lemon juice, nutritional yeast, garlic powder, salt, and pepper in a medium bowl, and mix well.
3. Divide the mixture between 6 cupcake molds.
4. Place the filled molds into the air fryer and Bake for 20 minutes, or until the tops are lightly browned and a toothpick inserted into the center comes out clean.
5. Serve cooled.

Variations & Ingredients Tips:

- Add sundried tomatoes, spinach or mushrooms to the veggie mix.
- Use another type of flour like oat or chickpea if needed.
- Top with avocado slices or salsa before serving.

Per Serving: Calories: 104; Total Fat: 2g; Saturated Fat: 0g; Cholesterol: 0mg; Sodium: 52mg; Total Carbs: 18g; Dietary Fiber: 3g; Total Sugars: 2g; Protein: 6g

Blueberry Muffins

Servings: 8 | Prep Time: 10 Minutes | Cooking Time: 14 Minutes

Ingredients:

- 1⅓ cups all-purpose flour
- ½ cup sugar
- 2 teaspoons baking powder
- ¼ teaspoon salt
- ⅓ cup canola oil
- 1 egg
- ½ cup milk
- ⅔ cup blueberries, fresh or frozen and thawed
- 8 foil muffin cups including paper liners

Directions:

1. Preheat air fryer to 165°C/330°F.
2. In a medium bowl, stir together flour, sugar, baking powder, and salt.
3. In a separate bowl, combine oil, egg, and milk and mix well.
4. Add egg mixture to dry ingredients and stir just until moistened.
5. Gently stir in blueberries.
6. Spoon batter evenly into muffin cups.
7. Place 4 muffin cups in air fryer basket and bake at 165°C/330°F for 14 minutes or until tops spring back when touched lightly.
8. Repeat previous step to cook remaining muffins.

Variations & Ingredients Tips:

- Use different berries like raspberries or blackberries.
- Add lemon or orange zest to the batter.
- Top with a streusel or crumb topping before baking.

Per Serving: Calories: 210; Total Fat: 9g; Saturated Fat: 1g; Cholesterol: 25mg; Sodium: 200mg; Total Carbs: 30g; Dietary Fiber: 1g; Total Sugars: 15g; Protein: 3g

Zucchini Hash Browns

Servings: 4 | Prep Time: 8 Minutes | Cooking Time: 20 Minutes

Ingredients:

- 2 shredded zucchinis
- 2 tbsp nutritional yeast
- 1 tsp allspice
- 1 egg white

Directions:

1. Preheat air fryer to 200°C/400°F.
2. Combine zucchinis, nutritional yeast, allspice, and egg white in a bowl.
3. Make 4 patties out of the mixture.
4. Cut 4 pieces of parchment paper, put a patty on

each, and fold in all sides to create a rectangle.

5. Using a spatula, flatten them and spread them out on the parchment.
6. Then unwrap each parchment and remove the hash browns onto the fryer and Air Fry for 12 minutes until golden brown and crispy, turning once.
7. Serve right away.

Variations & Ingredients Tips:

- Grate in carrots, onions or potatoes as well.
- Add shredded cheese or herbs like dill or parsley.
- Serve with salsa, sour cream or avocado on the side.

Per Serving: Calories: 41; Total Fat: 1g; Saturated Fat: 0g; Cholesterol: 0mg; Sodium: 34mg; Total Carbs: 6g; Dietary Fiber: 2g; Total Sugars: 3g; Protein: 4g

Blueberry Breakfast Cobbler

Servings: 4 | Preparation Time: 5 Minutes | Cooking Time:15 Minutes

Ingredients:

- 1/3 cup whole-wheat pastry flour
- 3/4 teaspoon baking powder
- Dash sea salt
- 1/2 cup 2% milk
- 2 tablespoons pure maple syrup
- 1/2 teaspoon vanilla extract
- Cooking oil spray
- 1/2 cup fresh blueberries
- 1/4 cup Granola, or plain store-bought granola

Directions:

1. In a medium bowl, whisk the flour, baking powder, and salt. Add the milk, maple syrup, and vanilla and gently whisk, just until thoroughly combined.
2. Preheat the unit by selecting BAKE, setting the temperature to 180°C/350°F, and setting the time to 3 minutes. Select START/STOP to begin.
3. Spray a 6-by-5-cm round baking pan with

cooking oil and pour the batter into the pan. Top evenly with the blueberries and granola.
4. Once the unitis preheated, place the pan into the basket.
5. Select BAKE, set the temperature to 180°C/350°F, and set the time to 15 minutes. Select START/STOP to begin.
6. When the cookingis complete, the cobbler should be nicely browned and a knife inserted into the middle should come out clean. Enjoy plain or topped with a little vanilla yogurt.

Variations & Ingredients Tips:

- The granola topping can be sprinkled over the berries before baking.
- Consider dusting with powdered sugar or serving with a dollop of yogurt or whipped cream if desired.

Per Serving: Calories: 112; Total fat: 1g; Saturated fat: <1g; Cholesterol: 3mg; Sodium: 69mg; Carbohydrates: 23g; Fiber: 2g; Protein: 3g

Quesadillas

Servings: 4 | Prep Time: 10 Minutes | Cooking Time: 12 Minutes

Ingredients:

- 4 eggs
- 2 tablespoons skim milk
- Salt and pepper
- Oil for misting or cooking spray
- 4 flour tortillas
- 4 tablespoons salsa
- 55g Cheddar cheese, grated
- 1/2 small avocado, peeled and thinly sliced

Directions:

1. Preheat air fryer to 135°C/270°F.
2. Beat together eggs, milk, salt and pepper.
3. Spray a 15x15cm air fryer baking pan lightly with cooking spray and add egg mixture.
4. Cook 9 mins, stirring every 1-2 mins, until eggs are scrambled. Remove and set aside.
5. Spray one side of each tortilla with oil or cooking spray. Flip over.

6. Divide eggs, salsa, cheese and avocado among tortillas, covering half of each.
7. Fold tortillas in half and press down lightly.
8. Place 2 tortillas in air fryer basket and cook at 200°C/390°F for 3 mins until crispy.
9. Repeat with remaining 2 tortillas.
10. Cut each quesadilla into halves or thirds before serving.

Variations & Ingredients Tips:

● Add cooked chorizo, chicken or peppers to the filling.
● Use whole wheat or veggie tortillas for extra nutrition.
● Serve with sour cream, guacamole or pico de gallo on the side.

Per Serving: Calories: 270; Total Fat: 14g; Saturated Fat: 4g; Cholesterol: 185mg; Sodium: 430mg; Total Carbs: 24g; Dietary Fiber: 3g; Sugars: 2g; Protein: 13g

the tahini mixture until they begin to soften and set aside on a plate.
5. Fill each wrap with ⅓ cup of the veggie mixture and wrap them into a roll.
6. Bake for 15 minutes until golden brown and crispy, turning once.
7. Serve right away.

Variations & Ingredients Tips:

● Use different types of vegetables, such as carrots or sweet potatoes, for a variety of flavors and textures.
● Add some chopped nuts or raisins to the filling for extra flavor and crunch.
● Serve the samosa rolls with a side of chutney or yogurt sauce for dipping.

Per Serving: Calories: 230; Total Fat: 5g; Saturated Fat: 1g; Cholesterol: 0mg; Sodium: 160mg; Total Carbs: 41g; Fiber: 6g; Sugars: 5g; Protein: 7g

Crispy Samosa Rolls

Servings: 4 | Prep Time: 20 Minutes | Cooking Time: 30 Minutes

Ingredients:

- ⅔ cup canned peas
- 4 scallions, finely sliced
- 2 cups grated potatoes
- 2 tablespoons lemon juice
- 1 teaspoon ground ginger
- 1 teaspoon curry powder
- 1 teaspoon Garam masala
- ¼ cup chickpea flour
- 1 tablespoon tahini
- 8 rice paper wrappers

Directions:

1. Preheat air fryer to 180°C/350°F.
2. Mix the peas, scallions, potatoes, lemon juice, ginger, curry powder, Garam masala, and chickpea flour in a bowl.
3. In another bowl, whisk tahini and 80 ml of water until combined. Set aside on a plate.
4. Submerge the rice wrappers, one by one, into

Morning Chicken Frittata Cups

Servings: 6 | Prep Time: 10 Minutes | Cooking Time: 30 Minutes

Ingredients:

- 1/4 cup shredded cooked chicken breast
- 3 eggs
- 2 tbsp heavy cream
- 4 tsp Tabasco sauce
- 1/4 cup grated Asiago cheese
- 2 tbsp chives, chopped

Directions:

1. Preheat air fryer to 175°C/350°F.
2. Beat all ingredients in a bowl.
3. Divide egg mixture between 6 greased muffin cups and place in air fryer basket.
4. Bake for 8-10 minutes until set.
5. Let cool slightly before serving.

Variations & Ingredients Tips:

● Use turkey, ham or bacon instead of chicken.

- Add sauteed vegetables like spinach, bell peppers or mushrooms.
- Substitute milk or almond milk for the heavy cream.

Per Serving: Calories: 110; Total Fat: 8g; Saturated Fat: 4g; Cholesterol: 120mg; Sodium: 260mg; Total Carbs: 1g; Dietary Fiber: 0g; Sugars: 0g; Protein: 8g

Baked Eggs

Servings: 4 | Prep Time: 5 Minutes | Cooking Time: 6 Minutes

Ingredients:

- 4 large eggs
- ⅛ teaspoon black pepper
- ⅛ teaspoon salt

Directions:

1. Preheat the air fryer to 165°C/330°F. Place 4 silicone muffin liners into the air fryer basket.
2. Crack 1 egg at a time into each silicone muffin liner. Sprinkle with black pepper and salt.
3. Bake for 6 minutes. Remove and let cool 2 minutes prior to serving.

Variations & Ingredients Tips:

- Add shredded cheese, chopped herbs or cooked meats on top of eggs before baking.
- Use ramekins or oven-safe bowls instead of silicone liners.

Per Serving: Calories: 70; Total Fat: 5g; Saturated Fat: 1.5g; Cholesterol: 185mg; Sodium: 115mg; Total Carbs: 0g; Dietary Fiber: 0g; Total Sugars: 0g; Protein: 6g

Cheesy Egg Bites

Servings: 6 | Prep Time: 10 Minutes | Cooking Time: 35 Minutes

Ingredients:

- ½ cup shredded Muenster cheese
- 5 eggs, beaten
- 3 tbsp sour cream
- ½ tsp dried oregano
- Salt and pepper to taste
- 1/3 cup minced bell pepper
- 3 tbsp minced scallions

Directions:

1. Preheat the air fryer to 163°C/325°F. Make a foil sling: Fold an 45-cm-long piece of heavy-duty aluminum foil lengthwise into thirds. Combine the eggs, sour cream, oregano, salt, and pepper in a bowl. Add the bell peppers, scallions, and cheese and stir. Add the mixture to 6 egg bite cups, making sure to get some of the solids in each cup.
2. Put the egg bite pan on the sling you made and lower it into the fryer. Leave the foil in but bend down the edges so they fit. Bake the bites for 10-15 minutes or until a toothpick inserted into the center comes out clean. Remove the egg bite pan using the foil sling. Cool for 5 minutes, then turn the pan upside down over a plate to remove the egg bites. Serve warm.

Variations & Ingredients Tips:

- Use different cheeses like cheddar or feta.
- Add cooked bacon, ham or sausage.
- Substitute yogurt for the sour cream.

Per Serving: Calories: 125; Total Fat: 8g; Saturated Fat: 4g; Cholesterol: 195mg; Sodium: 170mg; Total Carbs: 2g; Dietary Fiber: 0g; Total Sugars: 1g; Protein: 9g

Beef, Pork & Lamb Recipes

Lamb Meatballs With Quick Tomato Sauce

Servings: 4 | Prep Time: 20 Minutes | Cooking Time: 8 Minutes

Ingredients:

- ½ small onion, finely diced
- 1 clove garlic, minced
- 450 g ground lamb
- 2 tablespoons fresh parsley, finely chopped (plus more for garnish)
- 2 teaspoons fresh oregano, finely chopped
- 2 tablespoons milk
- 1 egg yolk
- Salt and freshly ground black pepper
- ½ cup crumbled feta cheese, for garnish
- Tomato Sauce:
- 2 tablespoons butter
- 1 clove garlic, smashed
- Pinch crushed red pepper flakes
- ¼ teaspoon ground cinnamon
- 1 (800 g) can crushed tomatoes
- Salt, to taste

Directions:

1. Combine all ingredients for the meatballs in a large bowl and mix just until everything is combined. Shape the mixture into 4 cm balls or shape the meat between two spoons to make quenelles (little three-sided footballs).
2. Preheat the air fryer to 200°C/400°F.
3. While the air fryer is preheating, start the quick tomato sauce. Place the butter, garlic and red pepper flakes in a sauté pan and heat over medium heat on the stovetop. Let the garlic sizzle a little, but before the butter starts to brown, add the cinnamon and tomatoes. Bring to a simmer and simmer for 15 minutes. Season to taste with salt (but not too much as the feta that you will be sprinkling on at the end will be salty).
4. Brush the bottom of the air fryer basket with a little oil and transfer the meatballs to the air fryer basket in one layer, air-frying in batches if necessary.
5. Air-fry at 200°C/400°F for 8 minutes, giving the basket a shake once during the cooking process to turn the meatballs over.
6. To serve, spoon a pool of the tomato sauce onto plates and add the meatballs in a decorative manner. Sprinkle the feta cheese on top and garnish with more fresh parsley. Serve immediately.

Variations & Ingredients Tips:

- Use different types of cheese, such as goat cheese or Parmesan, for a variety of flavors.
- Add some chopped Kalamata olives or capers to the tomato sauce for a briny flavor.
- Serve the meatballs with a side of pasta or crusty bread for a complete meal.

Per Serving: Calories: 510; Total Fat: 38g; Saturated Fat: 18g; Cholesterol: 170mg; Sodium: 780mg; Total Carbs: 15g; Fiber: 3g; Sugars: 8g; Protein: 31g

Garlic-buttered Rib Eye Steak

Servings: 2 | Prep Time: 5 Minutes | Cooking Time: 25 Minutes

Ingredients:

- 450g rib eye steak
- Salt and pepper to taste
- 1 tbsp butter
- 1 tsp paprika
- 1 tbsp chopped
- rosemary
- 2 garlic cloves, minced
- 2 tbsp chopped parsley
- 1 tbsp chopped mint

Directions:

1. Preheat air fryer to 200°C/400°F. Sprinkle salt

and pepper on both sides of the rib eye. Transfer the rib eye to the greased frying basket, then top with butter, mint, paprika, rosemary, and garlic. Bake for 6 minutes, then flip the steak. Bake for another 6 minutes. For medium-rare, the steak needs to reach an internal temperature of 60°C/140°F. Allow resting for 5 minutes before slicing. Serve sprinkled with parsley and enjoy!

Variations & Ingredients Tips:

- Use different compound butter flavors like blue cheese, horseradish or chipotle
- Slice the steak and serve over a salad for a lighter meal
- Top with sautéed mushrooms and onions for extra flavor

Per Serving: Calories: 594; Total Fat: 47g; Saturated Fat: 21g; Cholesterol: 156mg; Sodium: 194mg; Total Carbs: 2g; Dietary Fiber: 1g; Total Sugars: 0g; Protein: 41g

Brie And Cranberry Burgers

Servings: 3 | Prep Time: 15 Minutes | Cooking Time: 9 Minutes

Ingredients:

- 454g ground beef (80% lean)
- 1 tablespoon chopped fresh thyme
- 1 tablespoon Worcestershire sauce
- 1/2 teaspoon salt
- Freshly ground
- black pepper
- 1 (113g) wheel of Brie cheese, sliced
- Handful of arugula
- 3 or 4 brioche hamburger buns (or potato hamburger buns), toasted
- 57-114g whole berry cranberry sauce

Directions:

1. Combine the beef, thyme, Worcestershire sauce, salt and pepper together in a large bowl and mix well. Divide the meat into 4 (113g) portions or 3 larger portions and then form them into burger patties, being careful not to over-handle the meat.

2. Preheat the air fryer to 390°F/200°C and pour a little water into the bottom of the air fryer drawer. (This will help prevent the grease that drips into the bottom drawer from burning and smoking.)

3. Transfer the burgers to the air fryer basket. Air-fry the burgers at 390°F/200°C for 5 minutes. Flip the burgers over and air-fry for another 2 minutes. Top each burger with a couple slices of brie and air-fry for another minute or two, just to soften the cheese.

4. Build the burgers by placing a few leaves of arugula on the bottom bun, adding the burger and a spoonful of cranberry sauce on top. Top with the other half of the hamburger bun and enjoy.

Variations & Ingredients Tips:

- Use goat cheese or camembert instead of brie for a different flavor
- Add caramelized onions on top for extra flavor
- Brush the buns with garlic butter before toasting

Per Serving: Calories: 620; Total Fat: 32g; Saturated Fat: 14g; Cholesterol: 120mg; Sodium: 870mg; Total Carbs: 42g; Fiber: 2g; Sugars: 11g; Protein: 38g

Cajun Pork Loin Chops

Servings: 4 | Prep Time: 20 Minutes | Cooking Time: 25 Minutes

Ingredients:

- 8 thin boneless pork loin chops (около 680g total)
- 3.75ml Coarse sea salt
- 1 egg, beaten
- 5ml Cajun seasoning
- 120g bread crumbs
- 1 cucumber, sliced
- 1 tomato, sliced

Directions:

1. Place the chops between two sheets of parchment paper. Pound the pork to 6mm thickness using a meat mallet or rolling pin. Season with

sea salt. In a shallow bowl, beat the egg with 5ml of water and Cajun seasoning. In a second bowl, add the breadcrumbs. Dip the chops into the egg mixture, shake, and dip into the crumbs.

2. Preheat air fryer to 400°F/205°C. Place the chops in the greased frying basket and Air Fry for 6-8 minutes, flipping once until golden and cooked through. Serve immediately with cucumber and tomato.

Variations & Ingredients Tips:

- Use panko breadcrumbs instead of regular for an extra crispy coating
- Make a remoulade or comeback sauce for dipping
- Let the breaded chops rest for 10 minutes before frying for a better crust

Per Serving: Calories: 250; Total Fat: 8g; Saturated Fat: 2.5g; Cholesterol: 135mg; Sodium: 540mg; Total Carbs: 15g; Fiber: 1g; Sugars: 1g; Protein: 29g

Steakhouse Burgers With Red Onion Compote

Servings: 4 | Prep Time: 25 Minutes | Cooking Time: 22 Minutes

Ingredients:

- 680 g lean ground beef
- 2 cloves garlic, minced and divided
- 1 teaspoon Worcestershire sauce
- 1 teaspoon sea salt, divided
- ½ teaspoon black pepper
- 1 tablespoon extra-virgin olive oil
- 1 red onion, thinly sliced
- 59 g balsamic vinegar
- 1 teaspoon sugar
- 1 tablespoon tomato paste
- 2 tablespoons mayonnaise
- 2 tablespoons sour cream
- 4 brioche hamburger buns
- 1 cup arugula

Directions:

1. In a large bowl, mix together the ground beef, 1 of the minced garlic cloves, the Worcestershire sauce, ½ teaspoon of the salt, and the black pepper. Form the meat into 2.5 cm-thick patties. Make a dent in the center (this helps the center cook evenly). Let the meat sit for 15 minutes.

2. Meanwhile, in a small saucepan over medium heat, cook the olive oil and red onion for 4 minutes, stirring frequently to avoid burning. Add in the balsamic vinegar, sugar, and tomato paste, and cook for an additional 3 minutes, stirring frequently. Transfer the onion compote to a small bowl.

3. Preheat the air fryer to 175°C/350°F.

4. In another small bowl, mix together the remaining minced garlic, the mayonnaise, and the sour cream. Spread the mayo mixture on the insides of the brioche buns.

5. Cook the hamburgers for 6 minutes, flip the burgers, and cook an additional 2 to 6 minutes. Check the internal temperature to avoid under- or overcooking. Hamburgers should be cooked to at least 71°C/160°F. After cooking, cover with foil and let the meat rest for 5 minutes.

6. Meanwhile, place the buns inside the air fryer and toast them for 3 minutes.

7. To assemble the burgers, place the hamburger on one side of the bun, top with onion compote and 59 g arugula, and then place the other half of the bun on top.

Variations & Ingredients Tips:

- Mix some crumbled blue cheese or crispy bacon into the burger patties
- Top with sliced avocado, fried egg or sautéed mushrooms
- Swap arugula for watercress, baby spinach or butter lettuce

Per Serving: Calories: 588; Total Fat: 35g; Saturated Fat: 11g; Cholesterol: 124mg; Sodium: 945mg; Total Carbs: 32g; Dietary Fiber: 2g; Total Sugars: 10g; Protein: 39g

Cowboy Rib Eye Steak

Servings: 2 | Prep Time: 5 Minutes | Cooking Time: 20 Minutes

Ingredients:

- ¼ cup barbecue sauce
- 1 clove garlic, minced
- ⅛ teaspoon chili pepper
- ¼ teaspoon sweet paprika
- ¼ teaspoon cumin
- 1 rib-eye steak

Directions:

1. Preheat air fryer to 200°C/400°F.
2. In a bowl, whisk the barbecue sauce, garlic, chili pepper, paprika, and cumin. Divide in half and brush the steak with half of the sauce.
3. Add steak to the lightly greased frying basket and Air Fry for 10 minutes until you reach your desired doneness, turning once and brushing with the remaining sauce.
4. Let rest for 5 minutes onto a cutting board before slicing.
5. Serve warm.

Variations & Ingredients Tips:

- Use different types of steak, such as sirloin or tenderloin, for a variety of flavors and textures.
- Add some smoked paprika or chipotle pepper to the sauce for a smoky and spicy flavor.
- Serve the steak with a side of roasted potatoes or grilled asparagus for a complete meal.

Per Serving: Calories: 280; Total Fat: 16g; Saturated Fat: 6g; Cholesterol: 75mg; Sodium: 460mg; Total Carbs: 9g; Fiber: 0g; Sugars: 7g; Protein: 24g

Skirt Steak Fajitas

Servings: 4 | Prep Time: 20 Minutes | Cooking Time: 30 Minutes

Ingredients:

- 2 tablespoons olive oil
- ¼ cup lime juice
- 1 clove garlic, minced
- ½ teaspoon ground cumin
- ½ teaspoon hot sauce
- ½ teaspoon salt
- 2 tablespoons chopped fresh cilantro
- 454 g skirt steak
- 1 onion, sliced
- 1 teaspoon chili powder
- 1 red pepper, sliced
- 1 green pepper, sliced
- salt and freshly ground black pepper
- 8 flour tortillas
- shredded lettuce, crumbled Queso Fresco (or grated Cheddar cheese), sliced black olives, diced tomatoes, sour cream and guacamole for serving

Directions:

1. Combine the olive oil, lime juice, garlic, cumin, hot sauce, salt and cilantro in a shallow dish. Add the skirt steak and turn it over several times to coat all sides. Pierce the steak with a needle-style meat tenderizer or paring knife. Marinate the steak in the refrigerator for at least 3 hours, or overnight. When you are ready to cook, remove the steak from the refrigerator and let it sit at room temperature for 30 minutes.
2. Preheat the air fryer to 200°C/400°F.
3. Toss the onion slices with the chili powder and a little olive oil and transfer them to the air fryer basket. Air-fry at 200°C/400°F for 5 minutes. Add the red and green peppers to the air fryer basket with the onions, season with salt and pepper and air-fry for 8 more minutes, until the onions and peppers are soft. Transfer the vegetables to a dish and cover with aluminum foil to keep warm.
4. Place the skirt steak in the air fryer basket and pour the marinade over the top. Air-fry at 200°C/400°F for 12 minutes. Flip the steak over and air-fry at 200°C/400°F for an additional 5 minutes. (The time needed for your steak will depend on the thickness of the skirt steak. 17 minutes should bring your steak to roughly medium.) Transfer the cooked steak to a cutting board and let the steak rest for a few minutes. If the peppers and onions need to be heated, return them to the air fryer for just 1 to 2 minutes.
5. Thinly slice the steak at an angle, cutting against the grain of the steak. Serve the steak with the onions and peppers, the warm tortillas and the fajita toppings on the side so that everyone can make their own fajita.

- Use chicken, shrimp or portobello mushrooms instead of steak
- Add some sliced jalapeños or hot sauce for spice
- Serve with Spanish rice, refried beans and pico de gallo

Per Serving: Calories: 662; Total Fat: 32g; Saturated Fat: 10g; Cholesterol: 68mg; Sodium: 971mg; Total Carbs: 58g; Dietary Fiber: 4g; Total Sugars: 4g; Protein: 35g

Beef & Sauerkraut Spring Rolls

Servings: 4 | Prep Time: 15 Minutes | Cooking Time: 20 Minutes

Ingredients:

- 5 Colby cheese slices, cut into strips
- 2 tbsp Thousand Island Dressing for dipping
- 10 spring roll wrappers
- 115 g corned beef
- 2 cups sauerkraut
- 1 tsp ground cumin
- ½ tsp ground nutmeg
- 1 egg, beaten
- 1 tsp corn starch

Directions:

1. Preheat air fryer to 180°C/360°F. Mix the egg and cornstarch in a bowl to thicken. Lay out the spring roll wrappers on a clean surface. Place a few strips of the cut-up corned beef in the middle of the wraps. Sprinkle with Colby cheese, cumin, and nutmeg and top with 1-2 tablespoons of sauerkraut. Roll up and seal the seams with the egg and cornstarch mixture. Place the rolls in the greased frying basket. Bake for 7 minutes, shaking the basket several times until the spring rolls are golden brown. Serve warm with Thousand Island for dipping.

Variations & Ingredients Tips:

- Use Swiss cheese, Havarti, or Gruyere instead of Colby for a different flavor.
- Add chopped pickles, mustard, or Russian dressing to the filling for a Reuben-inspired twist.
- Serve with spicy brown mustard or horseradish sauce for dipping.

Per Serving: Calories: 272; Total Fat: 13g; Saturated Fat: 6g; Cholesterol: 75mg; Sodium: 1143mg; Total Carbohydrates: 26g; Dietary Fiber: 3g; Total Sugars: 3g; Protein: 13g

Easy-peasy Beef Sliders

Servings: 4 | Prep Time: 10 Minutes | Cooking Time: 25 Minutes

Ingredients:

- 454g ground beef
- 1/4 tsp cumin
- 1/4 tsp mustard powder
- 1/3 cup grated yellow onion
- 1/2 tsp smoked paprika
- Salt and pepper to taste

Directions:

1. Preheat air fryer to 175°C/350°F. Combine the ground beef, cumin, mustard, onion, paprika, salt, and black pepper in a bowl. Form mixture into 8 patties and make a slight indentation in the middle of each. Place beef patties in the greased frying basket and Air Fry for 8-10 minutes, flipping once. Serve right away and enjoy!

Variations & Ingredients Tips:

- Use ground turkey or chicken instead of beef
- Add shredded cheese like cheddar to the patty mixture
- Brush patties with BBQ sauce or garlic butter before serving

Per Serving: Calories: 265; Total Fat: 16g; Saturated Fat: 6g; Cholesterol: 75mg; Sodium: 185mg; Total Carbs: 2g; Dietary Fiber: 1g; Total Sugars: 1g; Protein: 26g

Greek-style Pork Stuffed Jalapeño Poppers

Servings: 6 | Prep Time: 20 Minutes | Cooking Time: 30 Minutes

Ingredients:

- 6 jalapeños, halved lengthwise
- 3 tbsp diced Kalamata olives
- 3 tbsp olive oil
- 113g ground pork
- 2 tbsp feta cheese
- 28g cream cheese, softened
- ½ tsp dried mint
- ½ cup Greek yogurt

Directions:

1. Warm 2 tbsp of olive oil in a skillet over medium heat. Stir in ground pork and cook for 6 minutes until no longer pink. Preheat air fryer to 175°C/350°F. Mix the cooked pork, olives, feta cheese, and cream cheese in a bowl. Divide the pork mixture between the peppers. Place them in the frying basket and Air Fry for 6 minutes. Mix the Greek yogurt with the remaining olive oil and mint in a small bowl. Serve with the poppers.

Variations & Ingredients Tips:

- Use stuffed banana peppers or mini bell peppers for a milder option
- Mix some chopped spinach or sun-dried tomatoes into the filling
- Drizzle with balsamic glaze before serving for a sweet and tangy finish

Per Serving: Calories: 207; Total Fat: 18g; Saturated Fat: 6g; Cholesterol: 34mg; Sodium: 347mg; Total Carbs: 3g; Dietary Fiber: 1g; Total Sugars: 2g; Protein: 8g

Leftover Roast Beef Risotto

Servings: 4 | Prep Time: 10 Minutes | Cooking Time: 30 Minutes

Ingredients:

- ½ chopped red bell pepper
- ½ chopped cooked roast beef
- 3 tablespoons grated Parmesan
- 2 teaspoons butter, melted
- 1 shallot, finely chopped
- 3 garlic cloves, minced
- ¾ cup short-grain rice
- 1¼ cups beef broth

Directions:

1. Preheat air fryer to 200°C/390°F. Add the melted butter, shallot, garlic, and red bell pepper to a baking pan and stir to combine. Air Fry for 2 minutes, or until the vegetables are crisp-tender.
2. Remove from the air fryer and stir in the rice, broth, and roast beef.
3. Put the cooking pan back into the fryer and Bake for 18-22 minutes, stirring once during cooking until the rice is al dente and the beef is cooked through.
4. Sprinkle with Parmesan and serve.

Variations & Ingredients Tips:

- Use different types of cheese, such as Gruyère or Asiago, for a variety of flavors.
- Add some sliced mushrooms or peas to the risotto for extra vegetables.
- Serve the risotto with a side of roasted asparagus or a green salad for a complete meal.

Per Serving: Calories: 280; Total Fat: 10g; Saturated Fat: 5g; Cholesterol: 45mg; Sodium: 530mg; Total Carbs: 29g; Fiber: 1g; Sugars: 2g; Protein: 17g

Sriracha Short Ribs

Servings: 4 | Prep Time: 5 Minutes | Cooking Time: 15 Minutes

Ingredients:

- 10 g sesame seeds
- 8 pork short ribs
- 118 g soy sauce
- 59 g rice wine vinegar
- 118 g chopped onion
- 2 garlic cloves, minced
- 15 g sesame oil
- 5 g sriracha
- 4 scallions, thinly

sliced
* Salt and pepper to taste

Directions:

1. Put short ribs in a resealable bag along with soy sauce, vinegar, onion, garlic, sesame oil, Sriracha, half of the scallions, salt, and pepper. Seal the bag and toss to coat. Refrigerate for one hour.
2. Preheat air fryer to 190°C/380°F. Place the short ribs in the air fryer. Bake for 8-10 minutes, flipping once until crisp. When the ribs are done, garnish with remaining scallions and sesame seeds. Serve and enjoy!

Variations & Ingredients Tips:

* Use beef short ribs or country-style pork ribs for meatier bites
* Brush the ribs with honey or brown sugar in the last few minutes of cooking for a sticky glaze
* Serve with kimchi, pickled radish and steamed rice

Per Serving: Calories: 535; Total Fat: 43g; Saturated Fat: 14g; Cholesterol: 113mg; Sodium: 2319mg; Total Carbs: 9g; Dietary Fiber: 1g; Total Sugars: 3g; Protein: 27g

Oktoberfest Bratwursts

Servings: 4 | Prep Time: 5 Minutes | Cooking Time: 35 Minutes

Ingredients:

* ½ onion, cut into half-moons
* 450 g pork bratwurst links
* 2 cups beef broth
* 1 cup beer
* 2 cups drained sauerkraut
* 2 tablespoons German mustard

Directions:

1. Pierce each bratwurst with a fork twice. Place them along with beef broth, beer, 1 cup of water, and onion in a saucepan over high heat and bring to a boil. Lower the heat and simmer for 15 minutes. Drain.
2. Preheat air fryer to 200°C/400°F. Place bratwursts and onion in the frying basket and Air Fry for 3 minutes. Flip bratwursts, add the sauerkraut and cook for 3 more minutes.
3. Serve warm with mustard on the side.

Variations & Ingredients Tips:

* Use different types of beer, such as lager or ale, for a variety of flavors.
* Add some sliced bell peppers or carrots to the bratwurst mixture for extra vegetables.
* Serve the bratwursts in buns with a side of German potato salad or soft pretzels for an authentic Oktoberfest meal.

Per Serving: Calories: 450; Total Fat: 32g; Saturated Fat: 11g; Cholesterol: 80mg; Sodium: 1620mg; Total Carbs: 15g; Fiber: 3g; Sugars: 4g; Protein: 21g

Air-fried Roast Beef With Rosemary Roasted Potatoes

Servings: 8 | Prep Time: 15 Minutes | Cooking Time: 60 Minutes

Ingredients:

* 2.25 kg top sirloin roast
* Salt and freshly ground black pepper
* 1 teaspoon dried thyme
* 900 g red potatoes,
* halved or quartered
* 2 teaspoons olive oil
* 1 teaspoon very finely chopped fresh rosemary, plus more for garnish

Directions:

1. Start by making sure your roast will fit into the air fryer basket without touching the top element. Trim it if you have to in order to get it to fit nicely in your air fryer. (You can always save the trimmings for another use, like a beef sandwich.)
2. Preheat the air fryer to 180°C/360°F.
3. Season the beef all over with salt, pepper and

thyme. Transfer the seasoned roast to the air fryer basket.

4. Air-fry at 180°C/360°F for 20 minutes. Turn the roast over and continue to air-fry at 180°C/360°F for another 20 minutes.

5. Toss the potatoes with the olive oil, salt, pepper and fresh rosemary. Turn the roast over again in the air fryer basket and toss the potatoes in around the sides of the roast. Air-fry the roast and potatoes at 180°C/360°F for another 20 minutes. Check the internal temperature of the roast with an instant-read thermometer, and continue to roast until the beef is 5° lower than your desired degree of doneness. (Rare - 55°C/130°F, Medium - 65°C/150°F, Well done - 75°C/170°F.) Let the roast rest for 5 to 10 minutes before slicing and serving. While the roast is resting, continue to air-fry the potatoes if desired for extra browning and crispiness.

6. Slice the roast and serve with the potatoes, adding a little more fresh rosemary if desired.

Variations & Ingredients Tips:

- Try using different cuts of beef, such as eye of round or tenderloin, for a variety of flavors and textures.
- Add some minced garlic or red pepper flakes to the potatoes for extra flavor.
- Serve the roast and potatoes with a side of horseradish sauce or gravy for a classic pairing.

Per Serving: Calories: 510; Total Fat: 25g; Saturated Fat: 9g; Cholesterol: 155mg; Sodium: 210mg; Total Carbs: 16g; Fiber: 2g; Sugars: 1g; Protein: 54g

Wasabi Pork Medallions

Servings: 4 | Prep Time: 10 Minutes | Cooking Time: 20 Minutes

Ingredients:

- 454g pork medallions
- 1 cup soy sauce
- 1 tbsp mirin
- 1/2 cup olive oil
- 3 cloves garlic, crushed
- 1 tsp fresh grated ginger
- 1 tsp wasabi paste

- 1 tbsp brown sugar

Directions:

1. Place all ingredients, except for the pork, in a resealable bag and shake to combine. Add the pork medallions to the bag, shake again, and place in the fridge to marinate for 2 hours. Preheat air fryer to 360°F/182°C. Remove pork medallions from the marinade and place them in the frying basket in rows. Air Fry for 14-16 minutes or until the medallions are cooked through and juicy. Serve.

Variations & Ingredients Tips:

- Use pork tenderloin instead of medallions and slice into medallions after cooking
- Add sliced green onions or sesame seeds as a garnish
- Substitute rice vinegar for the mirin for a different flavor

Per Serving: Calories: 430; Total Fat: 25g; Saturated Fat: 6g; Cholesterol: 90mg; Sodium: 2850mg; Total Carbs: 13g; Dietary Fiber: 1g; Total Sugars: 6g; Protein: 35g

Teriyaki Country-style Pork Ribs

Servings: 3 | Prep Time: 10 Minutes | Cooking Time: 30 Minutes

Ingredients:

- 3 tablespoons Regular or low-sodium soy sauce or gluten-free tamari sauce
- 3 tablespoons Honey
- 3/4 teaspoon
- Ground dried ginger
- 3/4 teaspoon Garlic powder
- 3 227g boneless country-style pork ribs
- Vegetable oil spray

Directions:

1. Preheat the air fryer to 350°F/177°C.
2. Mix the soy or tamari sauce, honey, ground ginger, and garlic powder in another bowl until

uniform.

3. Smear about half of this teriyaki sauce over all sides of the country-style ribs. Reserve the remainder of the teriyaki sauce. Generously coat the meat with vegetable oil spray.

4. When the machine is at temperature, place the country-style ribs in the basket with as much air space between them as possible. Air-fry undisturbed for 15 minutes. Turn the country-style ribs (but keep the space between them) and brush them all over with the remaining teriyaki sauce. Continue air-frying undisturbed for 15 minutes, or until an instant-read meat thermometer inserted into the center of one rib registers at least 145°F/63°C.

5. Use kitchen tongs to transfer the country-style ribs to a wire rack. Cool for 5 minutes before serving.

Variations & Ingredients Tips:

- Use boneless pork loin or tenderloin instead of country-style ribs
- Add crushed red pepper or sriracha to the teriyaki sauce for extra heat
- Sprinkle with sesame seeds or sliced green onions before serving

Per Serving: Calories: 525; Total Fat: 24g; Saturated Fat: 8g; Cholesterol: 155mg; Sodium: 790mg; Total Carbs: 30g; Dietary Fiber: 0g; Total Sugars: 24g; Protein: 44g

Sweet Potato–crusted Pork Rib Chops

Servings: 2 | Prep Time: 10 Minutes | Cooking Time: 14 Minutes

Ingredients:

- 2 Large egg white(s), well beaten
- 1½ cups (about 170 g) Crushed sweet potato chips (certified gluten-free, if a
- concern)
- 1 teaspoon Ground cinnamon
- 1 teaspoon Ground dried ginger
- 1 teaspoon Table salt (optional)
- 2 283 g, 2.5 cm-thick bone-in pork   rib chop(s)

Directions:

1. Preheat the air fryer to 190°C/375°F.

2. Set up and fill two shallow soup plates or small pie plates on your counter: one for the beaten egg white(s); and one for the crushed chips, mixed with the cinnamon, ginger, and salt (if using).

3. Dip a chop in the egg white(s), coating it on both sides as well as the edges. Let the excess egg white slip back into the rest, then set it in the crushed chip mixture. Turn it several times, pressing gently, until evenly coated on both sides and the edges. If necessary, set the chop aside and coat the remaining chop(s).

4. Set the chop(s) in the basket with as much air space between them as possible. Air-fry undisturbed for 12 minutes, or until crunchy and browned and an instant-read meat thermometer inserted into the center of a chop (without touching bone) registers 63°C/145°F. If the machine is at 180°C/360°F, you may need to add 2 minutes to the cooking time.

5. Use kitchen tongs to transfer the chop(s) to a wire rack. Cool for 2 or 3 minutes before serving.

Variations & Ingredients Tips:

- Use crushed tortilla chips, cornflakes or panko instead of sweet potato chips
- Add some smoked paprika or chili powder to the coating for extra kick
- Serve with roasted apples, sautéed spinach or mashed cauliflower

Per Serving: Calories: 541; Total Fat: 28g; Saturated Fat: 8g; Cholesterol: 141mg; Sodium: 926mg; Total Carbs: 30g; Dietary Fiber: 3g; Total Sugars: 8g; Protein: 44g

Argentinian Steak Asado Salad

Servings: 2 | Prep Time: 15 Minutes |

Cooking Time: 35 Minutes

Ingredients:

- 1 jalapeño pepper, sliced thin
- ¼ cup shredded pepper Jack cheese
- 1 avocado, peeled and pitted
- ¼ cup diced tomatoes
- ½ diced shallot
- 2 teaspoons chopped cilantro
- 2 teaspoons lime
- juice
- 400g flank steak
- 1 garlic clove, minced
- 1 teaspoon ground cumin
- Salt and pepper to taste
- ¼ lime
- 3 cups mesclun mix
- ½ cup pico de gallo

Directions:

1. Mash the avocado in a small bowl. Add tomatoes, shallot, cilantro, lime juice, salt, and pepper. Set aside.
2. Season the steak with garlic, salt, pepper, and cumin.
3. Preheat air fryer to 200°C/400°F. Put the steak into the greased frying basket. Bake 8-10 minutes, flipping once until your desired doneness. Remove and let rest. Squeeze the lime over the steak and cut into thin slices.
4. For one serving, plate half of mesclun, 2 tablespoons of cheese, and ¼ cup guacamole. Place half of the steak slices on top, then add ¼ cup pico de gallo and jalapeño if desired.

Variations & Ingredients Tips:

- Use different types of greens, such as romaine or spinach, for a variety of flavors and textures.
- Add some cooked black beans or corn for extra fiber and nutrients.
- For a spicier version, add some chipotle pepper or hot sauce to the guacamole or pico de gallo.

Per Serving: Calories: 460; Total Fat: 29g; Saturated Fat: 8g; Cholesterol: 100mg; Sodium: 630mg; Total Carbs: 17g; Fiber: 8g; Sugars: 5g; Protein: 38g

Effortless Beef & Rice

Servings: 4 | Prep Time: 10 Minutes | Cooking Time: 35 Minutes

Ingredients:

- 227g ground beef
- 1 onion, chopped
- 1 celery stalk, chopped
- 3 garlic cloves, minced
- 2 cups cooked rice
- 1 tomato, chopped
- 3 tbsp tomato paste
- 2/3 cup beef broth
- 1 tsp smoked paprika
- 1/2 tsp dried oregano
- 1/2 tsp ground nutmeg
- Salt and pepper to taste

Directions:

1. Preheat air fryer to 188°C/370°F.
2. In a baking pan, combine ground beef, onion, celery and garlic. Break up beef with a fork.
3. Place pan in greased air fryer basket and cook for 5-7 minutes until beef is browned.
4. Add rice, tomato, tomato paste, broth, paprika, oregano, nutmeg, salt and pepper to the pan. Stir well.
5. Return pan to air fryer and cook for 10-13 minutes, stirring once, until heated through and ingredients are blended.
6. Serve hot.

Variations & Ingredients Tips:

- Use ground turkey or chicken instead of beef.
- Add frozen mixed vegetables to increase nutrients.
- Top with shredded cheese before serving.

Per Serving: Calories: 295; Total Fat: 12g; Saturated Fat: 4g; Cholesterol: 50mg; Sodium: 460mg; Total Carbs: 28g; Dietary Fiber: 3g; Total Sugars: 5g; Protein: 18g

Pork & Beef Egg Rolls

Servings: 8 | Prep Time: 25 Minutes | Cooking Time: 8 Minutes

Ingredients:

- 115 g very lean ground beef
- 115 g lean ground pork
- 1 tablespoon soy sauce
- 1 teaspoon olive oil
- ½ cup grated carrots
- 2 green onions, chopped
- 2 cups grated Napa cabbage
- ¼ cup chopped water chestnuts
- ¼ teaspoon salt
- ¼ teaspoon garlic powder
- ¼ teaspoon black pepper
- 1 egg
- 1 tablespoon water
- 8 egg roll wraps
- Oil for misting or cooking spray

Directions:

1. In a large skillet, brown beef and pork with soy sauce. Remove cooked meat from skillet, drain, and set aside.
2. Pour off any excess grease from skillet. Add olive oil, carrots, and onions. Sauté until barely tender, about 1 minute.
3. Stir in cabbage, cover, and cook for 1 minute or just until cabbage slightly wilts. Remove from heat.
4. In a large bowl, combine the cooked meats and vegetables, water chestnuts, salt, garlic powder, and pepper. Stir well. If needed, add more salt to taste.
5. Beat together egg and water in a small bowl.
6. Fill egg roll wrappers, using about ¼ cup of filling for each wrap. Roll up and brush all over with egg wash to seal. Spray very lightly with olive oil or cooking spray.
7. Place 4 egg rolls in air fryer basket and cook at 200°C/390°F for 4 minutes. Turn over and cook 4 more minutes, until golden brown and crispy.
8. Repeat to cook remaining egg rolls.

Variations & Ingredients Tips:

- Use different types of vegetables, such as bean sprouts or bamboo shoots, for a variety of flavors and textures.
- Add some minced ginger or sesame oil to the filling for extra flavor.
- Serve the egg rolls with a side of sweet and sour sauce or hot mustard for dipping.

Per Serving: Calories: 200; Total Fat: 8g; Saturated Fat: 2g; Cholesterol: 50mg; Sodium: 470mg; Total Carbs: 21g; Fiber: 1g; Sugars: 1g; Protein: 11g

Poultry Recipes

Parmesan Chicken Fingers

Servings: 2 | Prep Time: 15 Minutes | Cooking Time: 19 Minutes

Ingredients:

- 1/2 cup flour
- 1 teaspoon salt
- Freshly ground black pepper
- 2 eggs, beaten
- 3/4 cup seasoned panko breadcrumbs
- 3/4 cup grated Parmesan cheese
- 8 chicken tenders (about 450g) OR 2 to 3 boneless, skinless chicken breasts, cut into strips
- Vegetable oil
- Marinara sauce

Directions:

1. Set up a dredging station. Combine the flour, salt and pepper in a shallow dish. Place the beaten eggs in second shallow dish, and combine the panko breadcrumbs and Parmesan cheese in a third shallow dish.
2. Dredge the chicken tenders in the flour mixture.

Then dip them into the egg, and finally place the chicken in the breadcrumb mixture. Press the coating onto both sides of the chicken tenders. Place the coated chicken tenders on a baking sheet until they are all coated. Spray both sides of the chicken fingers with vegetable oil.

3. Preheat the air fryer to 180°C/360°F.

4. Air-fry the chicken fingers in two batches. Transfer half the chicken fingers to the air fryer basket and air-fry for 9 minutes, turning the chicken over halfway through the cooking time. When the second batch of chicken fingers has finished cooking, return the first batch to the air fryer with the second batch and air-fry for one minute to heat everything through.

5. Serve immediately with marinara sauce, honey-mustard, ketchup or your favorite dipping sauce.

Variations & Ingredients Tips:

● Use almond flour and gluten-free breadcrumbs for a GF version.

● Add dried herbs or spices like oregano, paprika, or garlic powder to the breading.

● Serve over a salad or in a wrap with lettuce and tomato.

Per Serving: Calories: 600; Total Fat: 23g; Saturated Fat: 8g; Cholesterol: 270mg; Sodium: 1580mg; Total Carbs: 39g; Dietary Fiber: 2g; Total Sugars: 3g; Protein: 60g

Chicken & Fruit Biryani

Servings: 4 | Prep Time: 10 Minutes | Cooking Time: 30 Minutes

Ingredients:

● 3 chicken breasts, cubed
● 2 tsp olive oil
● 2 tbsp cornstarch
● 1 tbsp curry powder
● 1 apple, chopped
● ½ cup chicken broth
● 1/3 cup dried cranberries
● 1 cup cooked basmati rice

Directions:

1. Preheat air fryer to 190°C/380°F.

2. Combine the chicken and olive oil, then add some cornstarch and curry powder. Mix to coat, then add the apple and pour the mix in a baking pan.

3. Put the pan in the air fryer and Bake for 8 minutes, stirring once.

4. Add the chicken broth, cranberries, and 2 tbsp of water and continue baking for 10 minutes, letting the sauce thicken. The chicken should be lightly charred and cooked through.

5. Serve warm with basmati rice.

Variations & Ingredients Tips:

● Substitute chicken with cauliflower florets or paneer cheese for a vegetarian version.

● Use raisins, apricots, or figs instead of cranberries.

● Add a pinch of saffron or cardamom to the rice for extra aroma.

Per Serving: Calories: 350; Total Fat: 7g; Saturated Fat: 1g; Sodium: 250mg; Total Carbohydrates: 43g; Dietary Fiber: 4g; Total Sugars: 17g; Protein: 30g

Pickle Brined Fried Chicken

Servings: 4 | Prep Time: 20 Minutes (plus Brining Time) | Cooking Time: 47 Minutes

Ingredients:

● 4 bone-in, skin-on chicken legs, cut into drumsticks and thighs (about 1.6kg)
● Pickle juice from a 680g jar of kosher dill pickles
● 1/2 cup flour
● Salt and freshly ground black pepper
● 2 eggs
● 1 cup fine breadcrumbs
● 1 teaspoon salt
● 1 teaspoon freshly ground black pepper
● 1/2 teaspoon ground paprika
● 1/8 teaspoon ground cayenne pepper
● Vegetable or canola oil in a spray bottle

Directions:

1. Place the chicken in a shallow dish and pour the pickle juice over the top. Cover and transfer the chicken to the refrigerator to brine in the pickle juice for 3 to 8 hours.
2. When you are ready to cook, remove the chicken from the refrigerator to let it come to room temperature while you set up a dredging station. Place the flour in a shallow dish and season well with salt and freshly ground black pepper. Whisk the eggs in a second shallow dish. In a third shallow dish, combine the breadcrumbs, salt, pepper, paprika and cayenne pepper.
3. Preheat the air fryer to 190°C/370°F.
4. Remove the chicken from the pickle brine and gently dry it with a clean kitchen towel. Dredge each piece of chicken in the flour, then dip it into the egg mixture, and finally press it into the breadcrumb mixture to coat all sides of the chicken. Place the breaded chicken on a plate or baking sheet and spray each piece all over with vegetable oil.
5. Air-fry the chicken in two batches. Place two chicken thighs and two drumsticks into the air fryer basket. Air-fry for 10 minutes. Then, gently turn the chicken pieces over and air-fry for another 10 minutes. Remove the chicken pieces and let them rest on plate – do not cover. Repeat with the second batch of chicken, air-frying for 20 minutes, turning the chicken over halfway through.
6. Lower the temperature of the air fryer to 170°C/340°F. Place the first batch of chicken on top of the second batch already in the basket and air-fry for an additional 7 minutes.
7. Serve warm and enjoy.

Variations & Ingredients Tips:

● Use buttermilk instead of pickle juice for a traditional fried chicken brine.
● Add dried herbs like thyme, oregano or rosemary to the breading mix.
● Serve with hot sauce, honey or ranch dressing for dipping.

Per Serving: Calories: 620; Total Fat: 33g; Saturated Fat: 9g; Cholesterol: 295mg; Sodium: 2020mg; Total Carbs: 23g; Dietary Fiber: 1g; Total Sugars: 2g; Protein: 58g

Chicken Hand Pies

Servings: 8 | Prep Time: 20 Minutes | Cooking Time: 10 Minutes Per Batch

Ingredients:

● 3/4 cup chicken broth
● 3/4 cup frozen mixed peas and carrots
● 1 cup cooked chicken, chopped
● 1 tablespoon corn- starch
● 1 tablespoon milk
● Salt and pepper
● 1 8-count can organic flaky biscuits
● Oil for misting or cooking spray

Directions:

1. In a saucepan, bring broth to a boil. Add peas, carrots and chicken.
2. Mix cornstarch and milk, then stir into broth mixture until thickened.
3. Remove from heat, season with salt and pepper, and let cool slightly.
4. Separate biscuits into 16 rounds, flattening each slightly.
5. Place filling on 8 biscuit rounds. Top with remaining rounds and crimp edges sealed.
6. Mist both sides with oil or cooking spray.
7. Air fry in batches at 165°C/330°F for 10 minutes until golden brown.

Variations & Ingredients Tips:

● Use rotisserie or leftover chicken.
● Add diced potatoes, celery or onions to the filling.
● Brush with egg wash before cooking for a shiny finish.

Per Serving (2 hand pies): Calories: 312; Total Fat: 11g; Saturated Fat: 3g; Cholesterol: 38mg; Sodium: 779mg; Total Carbs: 41g; Dietary Fiber: 3g; Total Sugars: 4g; Protein: 13g

Thai Chicken Drumsticks

Servings: 4 | Prep Time: 10 Minutes + Marinating | Cooking Time: 20 Minutes

Ingredients:

- 2 tablespoons soy sauce
- 1/4 cup rice wine vinegar
- 2 tablespoons chili garlic sauce
- 2 tablespoons sesame oil
- 1 teaspoon minced fresh ginger
- 2 teaspoons sugar
- 1/2 teaspoon ground coriander
- Juice of 1 lime
- 8 chicken drumsticks (about 1.1kg)
- 1/4 cup chopped peanuts
- Chopped fresh cilantro
- Lime wedges

Directions:

1. Combine soy sauce, vinegar, chili sauce, oil, ginger, sugar, coriander and lime juice. Add drumsticks and marinate 30 mins.
2. Preheat air fryer to 190°C/370°F.
3. Place chicken in basket, spooning over half the marinade and reserving half.
4. Air fry 10 mins, turn and pour over remaining marinade. Cook 10 more mins.
5. Transfer chicken to plate and simmer marinade in a pan for 2 mins until thickened.
6. Serve chicken with thickened sauce, chopped peanuts, cilantro and lime wedges.

Variations & Ingredients Tips:

- Use chicken thighs instead of drumsticks.
- Add fish sauce or curry paste to the marinade.
- Serve over rice noodles or with a fresh salad.

Per Serving (2 drumsticks): Calories: 440; Total Fat: 27g; Saturated Fat: 6g; Cholesterol: 165mg; Sodium: 846mg; Total Carbs: 11g; Dietary Fiber: 1g; Total Sugars: 6g; Protein: 38g

Mexican Chicken Roll-ups

Servings: 4 | Prep Time: 15 Minutes | Cooking Time: 35 Minutes

Ingredients:

- 1/2 red bell pepper, cut into strips
- 1/2 green bell pepper, cut into strips
- 2 chicken breasts
- 1/2 lime, juiced
- 2 tbsp taco seasoning
- 1 spring onion, thinly sliced

Directions:

1. Preheat air fryer to 200°C/400°F.
2. Cut the chicken into cutlets by slicing the chicken breast in half horizontally in order to have 4 thin cutlets. Drizzle with lime juice and season with taco seasoning.
3. Divide the red pepper, green pepper, and spring onion equally between the 4 cutlets. Roll up the cutlets. Secure with toothpicks.
4. Place the chicken roll-ups in the air fryer and lightly spray with cooking oil. Bake for 12 minutes, turning once.
5. Serve warm.

Variations & Ingredients Tips:

- Add some shredded cheddar or pepper jack cheese inside the rolls.
- Serve with salsa, guacamole or sour cream for dipping.
- Use large lettuce leaves instead of bell peppers for a low-carb option.

Per Serving: Calories: 150; Total Fat: 3g; Saturated Fat: 0.5g; Cholesterol: 75mg; Sodium: 400mg; Total Carbs: 4g; Dietary Fiber: 1g; Total Sugars: 2g; Protein: 27g

Paprika Chicken Drumettes

Servings: 2 | Prep Time: 10 Minutes (plus Marinating Time) | Cooking Time: 30 Minutes

Ingredients:

- 450g chicken drumettes
- 1 cup buttermilk
- 3/4 cup bread crumbs
- 1/2 tsp smoked paprika
- 1 tsp chicken seasoning
- 1/2 tsp garlic powder
- Salt and pepper to taste
- 3 tsp lemon juice

Directions:

1. Mix drumettes and buttermilk in a bowl and let sit covered in the fridge overnight.
2. Preheat air fryer at 175°C/350°F.
3. In a shallow bowl, combine the remaining ingredients. Shake excess buttermilk off drumettes and dip them in the breadcrumb mixture.
4. Place breaded drumettes in the greased frying basket and Air Fry for 12 minutes.
5. Increase air fryer temperature to 200°C/400°F, toss chicken, and cook for 8 minutes.
6. Let rest for 5 minutes before serving.

Variations & Ingredients Tips:

● Use hot paprika or add cayenne for a spicy kick.
● Substitute buttermilk with Greek yogurt or sour cream.
● Serve with a cool ranch or blue cheese dipping sauce.

Per Serving: Calories: 540; Total Fat: 28g; Saturated Fat: 8g; Cholesterol: 200mg; Sodium: 850mg; Total Carbs: 29g; Dietary Fiber: 1g; Total Sugars: 5g; Protein: 45g

Chicken Rochambeau

Servings: 4 | Prep Time: 15 Minutes | Cooking Time: 20 Minutes

Ingredients:

- 1 tablespoon butter
- 4 chicken tenders, cut in half crosswise
- salt and pepper
- ¼ cup flour
- oil for misting
- 4 slices ham, 0.6- to 1-cm thick and large enough to cover an English muffin
- 2 English muffins, split

- Sauce
- 2 tablespoons butter
- ½ cup chopped green onions
- ½ cup chopped mushrooms
- 2 tablespoons flour
- 1 cup chicken broth
- ¼ teaspoon garlic powder
- 1 ½ teaspoons Worcestershire sauce

Directions:

1. Place 1 tablespoon of butter in air fryer baking pan and cook at 200°C/390°F for 2 minutes to melt.
2. Sprinkle chicken tenders with salt and pepper to taste, then roll in the ¼ cup of flour.
3. Place chicken in baking pan, turning pieces to coat with melted butter.
4. Cook at 200°C/390°F for 5 minutes. Turn chicken pieces over, and spray tops lightly with olive oil. Cook 5 minutes longer or until juices run clear. The chicken will not brown.
5. While chicken is cooking, make the sauce: In a medium saucepan, melt the 2 tablespoons of butter.
6. Add onions and mushrooms and sauté until tender, about 3 minutes.
7. Stir in the flour. Gradually add broth, stirring constantly until you have a smooth gravy.
8. Add garlic powder and Worcestershire sauce and simmer on low heat until sauce thickens, about 5 minutes.
9. When chicken is cooked, remove baking pan from air fryer and set aside.
10. Place ham slices directly into air fryer basket and cook at 200°C/390°F for 5 minutes or until hot and beginning to sizzle a little. Remove and set aside on top of the chicken for now.
11. Place the English muffin halves in air fryer basket and cook at 200°C/390°F for 1 minute.
12. Open air fryer and place a ham slice on top of each English muffin half. Stack 2 pieces of chicken on top of each ham slice. Cook at 200°C/390°F for 1 to 2 minutes to heat through.
13. Place each English muffin stack on a serving plate and top with plenty of sauce.

Variations & Ingredients Tips:

● Use turkey or pork instead of chicken for different meats.
● Substitute English muffins with biscuits or toast.
● Add a slice of cheese on top of the ham for extra richness.

Per Serving: Calories: 430; Total Fat: 24g; Saturated Fat: 11g; Sodium: 1070mg; Total Carbohydrates: 27g; Dietary Fiber: 2g; Total Sugars: 3g;

Protein: 29g

Tortilla Crusted Chicken Breast

Servings: 2 | Prep Time: 10 Minutes | Cooking Time: 12 Minutes

Ingredients:

- 1/3 cup flour
- 1 teaspoon salt
- 1 1/2 teaspoons chili powder
- 1 teaspoon ground cumin
- Freshly ground black pepper
- 1 egg, beaten
- 3/4 cup coarsely crushed yellow corn
- tortilla chips
- 2 (85-115g) boneless chicken breasts
- Vegetable oil
- 1/2 cup salsa
- 1/2 cup crumbled queso fresco
- Fresh cilantro leaves
- Sour cream or guacamole (optional)

Directions:

1. Set up 3 dishes: one with flour+salt+chili powder+cumin+pepper, one with beaten egg, one with crushed tortilla chips.
2. Dredge chicken in flour, then egg, then tortilla chips, pressing to adhere.
3. Spray chicken with oil on both sides.
4. Preheat air fryer to 195°C/380°F.
5. Air fry chicken for 6 mins, flip and cook 6 more mins.
6. Serve with salsa, queso fresco, cilantro, and sour cream/guacamole if desired.

Variations & Ingredients Tips:

- Use panko breadcrumbs instead of tortilla chips.
- Add lime zest or jalapeño to the breading.
- Serve with Mexican rice and beans on the side.

Per Serving: Calories: 471; Total Fat: 19g; Saturated Fat: 4g; Cholesterol: 200mg; Sodium: 1205mg; Total Carbs: 37g; Dietary Fiber: 3g; Total Sugars: 2g; Protein: 36g

Chicken Salad With Roasted Vegetables

Servings: 4 | Prep Time: 10 Minutes | Cooking Time: 25 Minutes

Ingredients:

- 4 tbsp honey-mustard salad dressing
- 3 chicken breasts, cubed
- 1 red onion, sliced
- 1 orange bell pepper, sliced
- 1 cup sliced zucchini
- ½ tsp dried thyme
- ½ cup mayonnaise
- 2 tbsp lemon juice

Directions:

1. Preheat air fryer to 200°C/400°F.
2. Add chicken, onion, pepper, and zucchini to the fryer. Drizzle with 1 tbsp of the salad dressing and sprinkle with thyme. Toss to coat.
3. Bake for 5-6 minutes. Shake the basket, then continue cooking for another 5-6 minutes.
4. In a bowl, combine the rest of the dressing, mayonnaise, and lemon juice.
5. Transfer the chicken and vegetables and toss to coat.
6. Serve and enjoy!

Variations & Ingredients Tips:

- Use a different dressing like ranch, Italian, or balsamic vinaigrette.
- Add cherry tomatoes, mushrooms, or eggplant to the vegetable mix.
- Serve over a bed of mixed greens or spinach for extra nutrients.

Per Serving: Calories: 420; Total Fat: 28g; Saturated Fat: 5g; Sodium: 420mg; Total Carbohydrates: 11g; Dietary Fiber: 2g; Total Sugars: 7g; Protein: 32g

Restaurant-style Chicken Thighs

Servings: 4 | Prep Time: 5 Minutes (plus 10 Minutes Marinating Time) | Cooking

Ingredients:

- 454 grams boneless, skinless chicken thighs
- ¼ cup barbecue sauce
- 2 cloves garlic, minced
- 1 tsp lemon zest
- 2 tbsp parsley, chopped
- 2 tbsp lemon juice

Directions:

1. Coat the chicken with barbecue sauce, garlic, and lemon juice in a medium bowl. leave to marinate for 10 minutes.
2. Preheat air fryer to 190°C/380°F.
3. When ready to cook, remove the chicken from the bowl and shake off any drips. Arrange the chicken in the air fryer and Bake for 16-18 minutes, until golden and cooked through.
4. Serve topped with lemon zest and parsley. Enjoy!

Variations & Ingredients Tips:

- Use honey mustard, teriyaki, or pesto sauce instead of BBQ for different flavors.
- Add sliced onions, peppers, or mushrooms to the marinade for extra veggies.
- Serve with sweet potato fries, coleslaw, or grilled corn on the side.

Per Serving: Calories: 250; Total Fat: 11g; Saturated Fat: 2.5g; Sodium: 440mg; Total Carbohydrates: 8g; Dietary Fiber: 0g; Total Sugars: 6g; Protein: 29g

Mumbai Chicken Nuggets

Servings: 4 | Prep Time: 15 Minutes | Cooking Time: 30 Minutes

Ingredients:

- 450g boneless, skinless chicken breasts
- 4 tsp curry powder
- Salt and pepper to taste
- 1 egg, beaten
- 2 tbsp sesame oil
- 1 cup panko bread crumbs
- 1/2 cup coconut yogurt
- 1/3 cup mango
- chutney
- 1/4 cup mayonnaise

Directions:

1. Preheat the air fryer to 200°C/400°F.
2. Cube the chicken into 5-cm pieces and sprinkle with 3 tsp of curry powder, salt, and pepper; toss to coat.
3. Beat together the egg and sesame oil in a shallow bowl and scatter the panko onto a separate plate. Dip the chicken in the egg, then in the panko, and press to coat. Lay the coated nuggets on a wire rack as you work.
4. Set the nuggets in the greased frying basket and Air Fry for 7-10 minutes, rearranging once halfway through cooking.
5. While the nuggets are cooking, combine the yogurt, chutney, mayonnaise, and the remaining teaspoon of curry powder in a small bowl.
6. Serve the nuggets with the dipping sauce.

Variations & Ingredients Tips:

- Use Greek yogurt instead of coconut yogurt for a tangy dip.
- Add some garam masala or cumin to the breading for extra flavor.
- Serve nuggets in naan bread or roti wraps with shredded veggies.

Per Serving: Calories: 450; Total Fat: 22g; Saturated Fat: 5g; Cholesterol: 150mg; Sodium: 470mg; Total Carbs: 30g; Dietary Fiber: 2g; Total Sugars: 15g; Protein: 36g

Prosciutto Chicken Rolls

Servings: 4 | Prep Time: 20 Minutes | Cooking Time: 30 Minutes

Ingredients:

- 1/2 cup chopped broccoli
- 1/2 cup grated cheddar
- 2 scallions, sliced
- 2 garlic cloves, minced
- 4 prosciutto thin slices
- 1/4 cup cream

- cheese
- Salt and pepper to taste
- 1/2 tsp dried oregano
- 1/2 tsp dried basil
- 4 chicken breasts
- 2 tbsp chopped cilantro

Directions:

1. Preheat air fryer to 190°C/375°F.
2. Combine broccoli, scallion, garlic, Cheddar, cream cheese, salt, pepper, oregano, and basil in a small bowl.
3. Prepare the chicken by placing it between two pieces of plastic wrap. Pound the chicken with a meat mallet or heavy can until it is evenly 1.25 cm thickness.
4. Top each with a slice of prosciutto and spoon 1/4 of the cheese mixture in the center of the chicken breast. Fold each breast over the filling and transfer to a greased baking dish.
5. Place the dish in the frying basket and bake for 8 minutes. Flip the chicken and bake for another 8-12 minutes.
6. Allow resting for 5 minutes. Serve warm sprinkled with cilantro and enjoy!

Variations & Ingredients Tips:

- Use spinach, sundried tomatoes or roasted red peppers in the filling.
- Wrap the chicken with bacon instead of prosciutto.
- Drizzle with a balsamic glaze before serving.

Per Serving: Calories: 340; Total Fat: 17g; Saturated Fat: 9g; Cholesterol: 145mg; Sodium: 610mg; Total Carbs: 3g; Dietary Fiber: 1g; Total Sugars: 1g; Protein: 42g

---

Pecan Turkey Cutlets

Servings: 4 | Prep Time: 15 Minutes | Cooking Time: 12 Minutes

Ingredients:

- 3/4 cup panko breadcrumbs
- 1/4 teaspoon salt
- 1/4 teaspoon pepper
- 1/4 teaspoon dry mustard

- 1/4 teaspoon poultry seasoning
- 1/2 cup pecans
- 1/4 cup cornstarch
- 1 egg, beaten
- 450g turkey cutlets, 1.3-cm thick
- Salt and pepper
- Oil for misting or cooking spray

Directions:

1. Place the panko crumbs, 1/4 teaspoon salt, 1/4 teaspoon pepper, mustard, and poultry seasoning in food processor. Process until crumbs are finely crushed. Add pecans and process in short pulses just until nuts are finely chopped. Go easy so you don't overdo it!
2. Preheat air fryer to 180°C/360°F.
3. Place cornstarch in one shallow dish and beaten egg in another. Transfer coating mixture from food processor into a third shallow dish.
4. Sprinkle turkey cutlets with salt and pepper to taste.
5. Dip cutlets in cornstarch and shake off excess. Then dip in beaten egg and roll in crumbs, pressing to coat well. Spray both sides with oil or cooking spray.
6. Place 2 cutlets in air fryer basket in a single layer and cook for 12 minutes or until juices run clear.
7. Repeat step 6 to cook remaining cutlets.

Variations & Ingredients Tips:

- Use walnuts, almonds or pistachios instead of pecans.
- Add some grated Parmesan to the breading mixture.
- Serve with a honey mustard or cranberry dipping sauce.

Per Serving: Calories: 320; Total Fat: 15g; Saturated Fat: 2g; Cholesterol: 100mg; Sodium: 330mg; Total Carbs: 17g; Dietary Fiber: 2g; Total Sugars: 1g; Protein: 31g

---

Thai Turkey And Zucchini Meatballs

Servings: 4 | Prep Time: 15 Minutes | Cooking Time: 12 Minutes

Ingredients:

- 1 1/2 cups grated zucchini, squeezed dry (about 1 large zucchini)
- 3 scallions, finely chopped
- 2 cloves garlic, minced
- 1 tablespoon grated fresh ginger
- 1 tablespoon finely chopped fresh cilantro
- Zest of 1 lime
- 1 teaspoon salt
- Freshly ground black pepper
- 680g ground turkey
- 2 eggs, lightly beaten
- 1 cup Thai sweet chili sauce
- Lime wedges, for serving

Directions:

1. Mix zucchini, scallions, garlic, ginger, cilantro, lime zest, salt, pepper, turkey and eggs.
2. Form into 24 golfball-sized meatballs.
3. Preheat air fryer to 195°C/380°F.
4. Air fry meatballs in batches for 12 mins, turning halfway.
5. Toss cooked meatballs in sweet chili sauce.
6. Serve over noodles/rice with extra sauce and lime wedges.

Variations & Ingredients Tips:

- Use ground chicken instead of turkey.
- Add shredded carrots or water chestnuts to the meatball mixture.
- Bake meatballs in oven at 400°F for 15-18 mins if no air fryer.

Per Serving (6 meatballs): Calories: 349; Total Fat: 14g; Saturated Fat: 3g; Cholesterol: 181mg; Sodium: 979mg; Total Carbs: 22g; Dietary Fiber: 1g; Total Sugars: 15g; Protein: 34g

Crunchy Chicken Strips

Servings: 4 | Prep Time: 15 Minutes | Cooking Time: 40 Minutes

Ingredients:

- 1 chicken breast, sliced into strips
- 1 tbsp grated Parmesan cheese
- 1 cup breadcrumbs
- 1 tbsp chicken seasoning
- 2 eggs, beaten
- Salt and pepper to taste

Directions:

1. Preheat air fryer to 180°C/350°F.
2. Mix the breadcrumbs, Parmesan cheese, chicken seasoning, salt, and pepper in a mixing bowl.
3. Coat the chicken with the crumb mixture, then dip in the beaten eggs. Finally, coat again with the dry ingredients.
4. Arrange the coated chicken pieces on the greased air fryer basket and Air Fry for 15 minutes. Turn over halfway through cooking and cook for another 15 minutes.
5. Serve immediately.

Variations & Ingredients Tips:

- Use panko breadcrumbs or crushed cornflakes for a crispier coating.
- Add garlic powder, onion powder, or paprika to the seasoning mix for extra flavor.
- Serve with honey mustard, ranch dressing, or ketchup for dipping.

Per Serving: Calories: 270; Total Fat: 8g; Saturated Fat: 2.5g; Sodium: 460mg; Total Carbohydrates: 22g; Dietary Fiber: 1g; Total Sugars: 2g; Protein: 25g

Popcorn Chicken Tenders With Vegetables

Servings: 4 | Prep Time: 15 Minutes | Cooking Time: 30 Minutes

Ingredients:

- 2 tbsp cooked popcorn, ground
- Salt and pepper to taste
- 450g chicken tenders
- 1/2 cup bread crumbs
- 1/2 tsp dried thyme
- 1 tbsp olive oil
- 2 carrots, sliced
- 12 baby potatoes

Directions:

1. Preheat air fryer to 190°C/380°F.

2. Season the chicken tenders with salt and pepper.
3. In a shallow bowl, mix the crumbs, popcorn, thyme, and olive oil until combined. Coat the chicken with mixture. Press firmly, so the crumbs adhere.
4. Arrange the carrots and baby potatoes in the greased frying basket and top them with the chicken tenders.
5. Bake for 9-10 minutes. Shake the basket and continue cooking for another 9-10 minutes, until the vegetables are tender.
6. Serve and enjoy!

Variations & Ingredients Tips:

- Use crushed corn flakes or potato chips instead of popcorn.
- Add some garlic powder, paprika or parmesan to the breading.
- Serve with honey mustard, BBQ sauce or ranch for dipping.

Per Serving: Calories: 320; Total Fat: 9g; Saturated Fat: 1.5g; Cholesterol: 85mg; Sodium: 280mg; Total Carbs: 30g; Dietary Fiber: 3g; Total Sugars: 2g; Protein: 31g

Italian Roasted Chicken Thighs

Servings: 6 | Prep Time: 5 Minutes | Cooking Time: 14 Minutes

Ingredients:

- 6 boneless chicken thighs
- 1/2 teaspoon dried oregano
- 1/2 teaspoon garlic powder
- 1/2 teaspoon sea

- salt
- 1/2 teaspoon black pepper
- 1/4 teaspoon crushed red pepper flakes

Directions:

1. Pat the chicken thighs with paper towel.
2. In a small bowl, mix the oregano, garlic powder, salt, pepper, and crushed red pepper flakes.

Rub the spice mixture onto the chicken thighs.
3. Preheat the air fryer to 200°C/400°F.
4. Place the chicken thighs in the air fryer basket and spray with cooking spray. Cook for 10 minutes, turn over, and cook another 4 minutes. When cooking completes, the internal temperature should read 75°C/165°F.

Variations & Ingredients Tips:

- Add some grated lemon zest to the spice mix for a bright flavor.
- Wrap each thigh with a slice of prosciutto before air frying.
- Serve over pasta, salad or roasted vegetables.

Per Serving: Calories: 210; Total Fat: 11g; Saturated Fat: 3g; Cholesterol: 140mg; Sodium: 390mg; Total Carbs: 0g; Dietary Fiber: 0g; Total Sugars: 0g; Protein: 28g

Asian-style Orange Chicken

Servings: 4 | Prep Time: 15 Minutes | Cooking Time: 25 Minutes

Ingredients:

- 454 grams chicken breasts, cubed
- Salt and pepper to taste
- 6 tbsp cornstarch
- 1 cup orange juice
- ¼ cup orange mar-
- malade
- ¼ cup ketchup
- ½ tsp ground ginger
- 2 tbsp soy sauce
- 1 1/3 cups edamame beans

Directions:

1. Preheat the air fryer to 190°C/375°F.
2. Sprinkle the chicken cubes with salt and pepper. Coat with 4 tbsp of cornstarch and set aside on a wire rack.
3. Mix the orange juice, marmalade, ketchup, ginger, soy sauce, and the remaining cornstarch in a cake pan, then stir in the beans.
4. Set the pan in the air fryer basket and Bake for 5-8 minutes, stirring once during cooking until the sauce is thick and bubbling. Remove from the fryer and set aside.

5. Put the chicken in the air fryer basket and fry for 10-12 minutes, shaking the basket once.
6. Stir the chicken into the sauce and beans in the pan. Return to the fryer and reheat for 2 minutes.

Variations & Ingredients Tips:

● Substitute chicken with tofu or shrimp for different protein options.
● Add sliced bell peppers, carrots, or broccoli to the sauce for extra veggies.
● Serve over steamed rice, quinoa, or noodles for a complete meal.

Per Serving: Calories: 400; Total Fat: 6g; Saturated Fat: 1g; Sodium: 830mg; Total Carbohydrates: 52g; Dietary Fiber: 5g; Total Sugars: 25g; Protein: 34g

Turkey-hummus Wraps

Servings: 4 | Prep Time: 10 Minutes | Cooking Time: 7 Minutes Per Batch

Ingredients:

● 4 large whole wheat wraps
● ½ cup hummus
● 16 thin slices deli turkey
● 8 slices provolone cheese
● 1 cup fresh baby spinach (or more to taste)

Directions:

1. To assemble, place 2 tablespoons of hummus on each wrap and spread to within about 25 cm from edges. Top with 4 slices of turkey and 2 slices of provolone. Finish with 1/4 cup of baby spinach—or pile on as much as you like.
2. Roll up each wrap. You don't need to fold or seal the ends.
3. Place 2 wraps in air fryer basket, seam side down.
4. Cook at 180°C/360°F for 4 minutes to warm filling and melt cheese. If you like, you can continue cooking for 3 more minutes, until the wrap is slightly crispy.
5. Repeat step 4 to cook remaining wraps.

Variations & Ingredients Tips:

● Use flavored hummus like roasted red pepper or garlic.
● Add sliced cucumbers, tomatoes or roasted veggies.
● Make it vegetarian by using sliced feta or fresh mozzarella instead of turkey.

Per Serving: Calories: 420; Total Fat: 18g; Saturated Fat: 8g; Cholesterol: 55mg; Sodium: 1260mg; Total Carbs: 42g; Dietary Fiber: 5g; Total Sugars: 6g; Protein: 28g

Fish And Seafood Recipes

Halibut Quesadillas

Servings: 2 | Prep Time: 15 Minutes | Cooking Time: 30 Minutes

Ingredients:

● 1/4 cup shredded cheddar
● 1/4 cup shredded mozzarella
● 1 tsp olive oil
● 2 tortilla shells
● 1 halibut fillet
● 1/2 peeled avocado, sliced
● 1 garlic clove, minced
● Salt and pepper to taste
● 1/2 tsp lemon juice

Directions:

1. Preheat air fryer to 175°C/350°F.
2. Brush the halibut fillet with olive oil and sprinkle with salt and pepper. Bake in the air fryer for 12-14 minutes, flipping once until cooked through.
3. Combine the avocado, garlic, salt, pepper, and lemon juice in a bowl and, using a fork, mash lightly until the avocado is slightly chunky.
4. Add and spread the resulting guacamole on one tortilla. Top with the cooked fish and cheeses, and cover with the second tortilla.
5. Bake in the air fryer 6-8, flipping once until the cheese is melted.
6. Serve immediately.

Variations & Ingredients Tips:

● Use tilapia, cod or mahi mahi instead of halibut.
● Add some sautéed bell peppers, onions or mushrooms.
● Serve with salsa, sour cream and hot sauce on the side.

Per Serving: Calories: 410; Total Fat: 21g; Saturated Fat: 7g; Cholesterol: 75mg; Sodium: 550mg; Total Carbs: 28g; Dietary Fiber: 5g; Total Sugars: 1g; Protein: 31g

---

Catalan Sardines With Romesco Sauce

Servings:2 | Prep Time: 5 Minutes | Cooking Time: 15 Minutes

Ingredients:

● 2 cans skinless, boneless sardines in oil, drained
● ½ cup warmed romesco sauce
● ½ cup bread crumbs

Directions:

1. Preheat air fryer to 180°C/350°F.
2. In a shallow dish, add bread crumbs. Roll in sardines to coat.
3. Place sardines in the greased air fryer basket and Air Fry for 6 minutes, turning once.
4. Serve with romesco sauce.

Variations & Ingredients Tips:

● Use canned mackerel, anchovies, or smoked trout instead of sardines.
● Make your own romesco sauce by blending roasted red peppers, tomatoes, garlic, almonds, and olive oil.
● Serve on top of toast points, crackers, or a bed of salad greens.

Per Serving: Calories: 360; Total Fat: 24g; Saturated Fat: 4g; Sodium: 680mg; Total Carbohydrates: 22g; Dietary Fiber: 2g; Total Sugars: 4g; Protein: 18g

---

Buttered Swordfish Steaks

Servings: 4 | Prep Time: 15 Minutes | Cooking Time: 30 Minutes

Ingredients:

● 4 swordfish steaks
● 2 eggs, beaten
● 85 grams melted butter
● ½ cup breadcrumbs
● Black pepper to taste
● 1 tsp dried rosemary
● 1 tsp dried marjoram
● 1 lemon, cut into wedges

Directions:

1. Preheat air fryer to 180°C/350°F.
2. Place the eggs and melted butter in a bowl and stir thoroughly.
3. Combine the breadcrumbs, rosemary, marjoram, and black pepper in a separate bowl.
4. Dip the swordfish steaks in the beaten eggs, then coat with the crumb mixture.
5. Place the coated fish in the air fryer basket.
6. Air Fry for 12-14 minutes, turning once until the fish is cooked through and the crust is toasted and crispy.
7. Serve with lemon wedges.

Variations & Ingredients Tips:

- Use cod, halibut, or mahi-mahi instead of swordfish for different fish options.
- Add grated Parmesan cheese or finely chopped nuts to the breading for extra flavor and texture.
- Serve with tartar sauce, garlic aioli, or a side of roasted vegetables.

Per Serving: Calories: 420; Total Fat: 27g; Saturated Fat: 15g; Sodium: 330mg; Total Carbohydrates: 11g; Dietary Fiber: 1g; Total Sugars: 1g; Protein: 33g

Mahi-mahi "burrito" Fillets

Servings: 3 | Prep Time: 10 Minutes | Cooking Time: 10 Minutes

Ingredients:

- 1 Large egg white
- 1½ cups (170g) Crushed corn tortilla chips (gluten-free, if a concern)
- 1 tablespoon Chile powder
- 3 (150g) skinless mahi-mahi fillets
- 6 tablespoons Canned refried beans
- Vegetable oil spray

Directions:

1. Preheat the air fryer to 200°C/400°F.
2. Set up and fill two shallow plates: one with the egg white, beaten until foamy; and one with the crushed tortilla chips.
3. Gently rub 1/2 teaspoon chile powder on each side of each fillet.
4. Spread 1 tablespoon refried beans over both sides and edges of each fillet.
5. Dip the fillet in the egg white, turning to coat both sides. Let excess egg white drip off, then coat in crushed tortilla chips, pressing gently.
6. Coat the fillet all over with vegetable oil spray, then set aside. Prepare remaining fillets the same way.
7. Set fillets in air fryer basket with space between them. Air-fry for 10 mins until crisp and browned.
8. Transfer to a plate and let cool for 1 minute before serving hot.

Variations & Ingredients Tips:

- Use gluten-free tortilla chips if needed.
- Add lime zest or chili powder to the refried beans.
- Serve with salsa, guacamole, sour cream.

Per Serving: Calories: 290; Total Fat: 11g; Saturated Fat: 2g; Cholesterol: 50mg; Sodium: 500mg; Total Carbs: 25g; Dietary Fiber: 3g; Total Sugars: 1g; Protein: 24g

French Grouper Nicoise

Servings: 4 | Prep Time: 10 Minutes | Cooking Time: 20 Minutes

Ingredients:

- 4 grouper fillets
- Salt to taste
- 1/2 tsp ground cumin
- 3 garlic cloves, minced
- 1 tomato, sliced
- 1/4 cup sliced Nicoise olives
- 1/4 cup dill, chopped
- 1 lemon, juiced
- 1/4 cup olive oil

Directions:

1. Preheat air fryer to 195°C/380°F.
2. Season grouper fillets with salt and cumin.
3. Arrange fillets in greased air fryer basket.
4. Top with garlic, tomato, olives and fresh dill.
5. Drizzle with lemon juice and olive oil.
6. Bake for 10-12 minutes.
7. Serve and enjoy!

Variations & Ingredients Tips:

- Use other white fish like halibut or cod.
- Add capers, red onion or roasted red peppers.
- Serve over arugula or with roasted potatoes.

Per Serving: Calories: 275; Total Fat: 13g; Saturated Fat: 2g; Cholesterol: 86mg; Sodium: 267mg; Total Carbs: 3g; Dietary Fiber: 1g; Total Sugars: 0g; Protein: 35g

Family Fish Nuggets With Tartar Sauce

Servings: 4 | Prep Time: 15 Minutes | Cooking Time: 30 Minutes

Ingredients:

- 1/2 cup mayonnaise
- 1 tbsp yellow mustard
- 1/2 cup diced dill pickles
- Salt and pepper to taste
- 1 egg, beaten
- 1/4 cup cornstarch
- 1/4 cup flour
- 450g cod, cut into sticks

Directions:

1. Make tartar sauce by mixing mayo, mustard, pickles, salt and pepper. Set aside.
2. Preheat air fryer to 175°C/350°F.
3. Set up 2 bowls: one with beaten egg, one with combined cornstarch, flour, salt and pepper.
4. Dip fish sticks in egg, then coat in flour mixture.
5. Arrange fish in greased air fryer basket and cook for 10 mins, flipping once.
6. Serve fish nuggets with tartar sauce for dipping.

Variations & Ingredients Tips:

- Use any firm white fish like cod, haddock or halibut.
- Add panko breadcrumbs to the coating for extra crunch.
- Serve with lemon wedges or malt vinegar on the side.

Per Serving: Calories: 299; Total Fat: 12g; Saturated Fat: 2g; Cholesterol: 118mg; Sodium: 429mg; Total Carbs: 23g; Dietary Fiber: 1g; Total Sugars: 3g; Protein: 24g

Timeless Garlic-lemon Scallops

Servings: 2 | Prep Time: 5 Minutes | Cooking Time: 15 Minutes

Ingredients:

- 2 tbsp butter, melted
- 1 garlic clove, minced
- 1 tbsp lemon juice
- 450g jumbo sea scallops

Directions:

1. Preheat air fryer to 200°C/400°F.
2. Whisk butter, garlic, and lemon juice in a bowl. Roll scallops in the mixture to coat all sides.
3. Place scallops in the frying basket and Air Fry for 4 minutes, flipping once. Brush the tops of each scallop with butter mixture and cook for 4 more minutes, flipping once.
4. Serve and enjoy!

Variations & Ingredients Tips:

- Sprinkle scallops with Old Bay seasoning or smoked paprika.
- Wrap each scallop with a slice of prosciutto before air frying.
- Serve over angel hair pasta or creamy risotto.

Per Serving: Calories: 290; Total Fat: 16g; Saturated Fat: 9g; Cholesterol: 100mg; Sodium: 990mg; Total Carbs: 5g; Dietary Fiber: 0g; Total Sugars: 0g; Protein: 33g

British Fish & Chips

Servings: 4 | Prep Time: 20 Minutes | Cooking Time: 40 Minutes

Ingredients:

- 2 peeled russet potatoes, thinly sliced
- 1 egg white
- 1 tbsp lemon juice
- 1/3 cup ground almonds
- 2 bread slices, crumbled
- 1/2 tsp dried basil
- 4 haddock fillets

Directions:

1. Preheat air fryer to 200°C/390°F.
2. Lay the potato slices in the frying basket and Air Fry for 11-15 minutes. Turn the fries a couple of times while cooking.

3. While the fries are cooking, whisk the egg white and lemon juice together in a bowl. On a plate, combine the almonds, breadcrumbs, and basil.
4. First, one at a time, dip the fillets into the egg mix and then coat in the almond/breadcrumb mix. Lay the fillets on a wire rack until the fries are done.
5. Preheat the oven to 175°C/350°F. After the fries are done, move them to a pan and place in the oven to keep warm.
6. Put the fish in the frying basket and Air Fry for 10-14 minutes or until cooked through, golden, and crispy.
7. Serve with the fries.

Variations & Ingredients Tips:

● Use cod, pollock or halibut instead of haddock.
● Season the fish batter with salt, pepper and Old Bay seasoning.
● Serve with malt vinegar, tartar sauce and mushy peas.

Per Serving: Calories: 400; Total Fat: 17g; Saturated Fat: 2g; Cholesterol: 80mg; Sodium: 260mg; Total Carbs: 34g; Dietary Fiber: 5g; Total Sugars: 2g; Protein: 31g

Bacon-wrapped Scallops

Servings: 4 | Prep Time: 10 Minutes | Cooking Time: 8 Minutes

Ingredients:

● 16 large scallops
● 8 bacon strips
● 1/2 teaspoon black

pepper
● 1/4 teaspoon smoked paprika

Directions:

1. Pat the scallops dry with a paper towel. Slice each of the bacon strips in half. Wrap 1 bacon strip around 1 scallop and secure with a toothpick. Repeat with the remaining scallops. Season the scallops with pepper and paprika.
2. Preheat the air fryer to 175°C/350°F.
3. Place the bacon-wrapped scallops in the air fry-

er basket and cook for 4 minutes, shake the basket, cook another 3 minutes, shake the basket, and cook another 1 to 3 to minutes. When the bacon is crispy, the scallops should be cooked through and slightly firm, but not rubbery.
4. Serve immediately.

Variations & Ingredients Tips:

● Brush the scallops with a mixture of melted butter, garlic and lemon juice before wrapping.
● Sprinkle with chopped fresh parsley or chives before serving.
● Serve with a lemon wedge and tartar sauce on the side.

Per Serving: Calories: 180; Total Fat: 9g; Saturated Fat: 3g; Cholesterol: 50mg; Sodium: 620mg; Total Carbs: 2g; Dietary Fiber: 0g; Total Sugars: 0g; Protein: 21g

Mojito Fish Tacos

Servings: 4 | Prep Time: 15 Minutes | Cooking Time: 30 Minutes

Ingredients:

● 1 1/2 cups chopped red cabbage
● 450g cod fillets
● 2 tsp olive oil
● 3 tbsp lemon juice
● 1 large carrot, grat-

ed
● 1 tbsp white rum
● 1/2 cup salsa
● 1/3 cup Greek yogurt
● 4 soft tortillas

Directions:

1. Preheat air fryer to 200°C/390°F.
2. Rub the fish with olive oil, then a splash with 1 tbsp of lemon juice.
3. Place in the fryer and Air Fry for 9-12 minutes. The fish should flake when done.
4. Mix the remaining 2 tbsp lemon juice, red cabbage, carrots, salsa, rum, and yogurt in a bowl.
5. Take the fish out of the fryer and tear into large pieces.
6. Serve with tortillas and cabbage mixture. Enjoy!

Variations & Ingredients Tips:

- Use other white fish like tilapia or mahi mahi.
- Add diced mango or pineapple to the cabbage slaw.
- Drizzle with extra lime juice and chopped cilantro.

Per Serving: Calories: 255; Total Fat: 4g; Saturated Fat: 1g; Cholesterol: 60mg; Sodium: 360mg; Total Carbs: 25g; Fiber: 3g; Sugars: 6g; Protein: 29g

Salty German-style Shrimp Pancakes

Servings: 4 | Prep Time: 5 Minutes | Cooking Time: 15 Minutes

Ingredients:

- 1 tbsp butter
- 3 eggs, beaten
- 1/2 cup flour
- 1/2 cup milk
- 1/8 tsp salt
- 1 cup salsa
- 1 cup cooked shrimp, minced
- 2 tbsp cilantro, chopped

Directions:

1. Preheat air fryer to 200°C/390°F.
2. Mix the eggs, flour, milk, and salt in a bowl until frothy.
3. Pour the batter into a greased baking pan and place in the air fryer.
4. Bake for 15 minutes or until the pancake is puffed and golden.
5. Flip the pancake onto a plate.
6. Mix salsa, shrimp, and cilantro. Top the pancake and serve.

Variations & Ingredients Tips:

- Add diced onions, peppers or spinach to the batter.
- Use corn or whole wheat flour for extra nutrition.
- Serve with sour cream, guacamole or hot sauce.

Per Serving: Calories: 200; Total Fat: 7g; Saturated Fat: 3g; Cholesterol: 190mg; Sodium: 570mg; Total Carbs: 20g; Dietary Fiber: 2g; Sugars: 3g; Protein: 13g

Herb-rubbed Salmon With Avocado

Servings: 4 | Prep Time: 15 Minutes | Cooking Time: 30 Minutes

Ingredients:

- 1 tbsp sweet paprika
- 1/2 tsp cayenne pepper
- 1 tsp garlic powder
- 1 tsp dried oregano
- 1/2 tsp dried coriander
- 1 tsp dried thyme
- 1/2 tsp dried dill
- Salt and pepper to taste
- 4 wild salmon fillets
- 2 tbsp chopped red onion
- 1 1/2 tbsp fresh lemon juice
- 1 tsp olive oil
- 2 tbsp cilantro, chopped
- 1 avocado, diced

Directions:

1. Mix spices, salt and pepper in a bowl. Rub salmon fillets with oil and coat with spice mix.
2. In another bowl, mix onion, lemon juice, oil, cilantro, salt and pepper. Let sit 5 mins then add avocado.
3. Preheat air fryer to 200°C/400°F.
4. Place salmon skin-side down in greased basket and bake 5-7 mins until flaky.
5. Transfer to a plate and top with avocado salsa.

Variations & Ingredients Tips:

- Use other fresh herbs like parsley or chives in the salsa.
- Add lime juice or hot sauce to the salsa for extra flavor.
- Serve salmon over greens or cauliflower rice.

Per Serving: Calories: 393; Total Fat: 24g; Saturated Fat: 4g; Cholesterol: 94mg; Sodium: 167mg; Total Carbs: 11g; Dietary Fiber: 6g; Total Sugars: 1g; Protein: 35g

Caribbean Skewers

Ingredients:

- 680 grams large shrimp, peeled and deveined
- 1 can pineapple chunks, drained, liquid reserved
- 1 red bell pepper, chopped
- 3 scallions, chopped
- 1 tbsp lemon juice
- 1 tbsp olive oil
- ½ tsp jerk seasoning
- ⅛ tsp cayenne pepper
- 2 tbsp cilantro, chopped

Directions:

1. Preheat the air fryer to 190°C/375°F.
2. Thread the shrimp, pineapple, bell pepper, and scallions onto 8 bamboo skewers.
3. Mix 3 tbsp of pineapple juice with lemon juice, olive oil, jerk seasoning, and cayenne pepper. Brush every bit of the mix over the skewers.
4. Place 4 kebabs in the air fryer basket, add a rack, and put the rest of the skewers on top.
5. Bake for 6-9 minutes and rearrange at about 4-5 minutes. Cook until the shrimp curl and pinken.
6. Sprinkle with freshly chopped cilantro and serve.

Variations & Ingredients Tips:

- Use chicken, beef, or tofu instead of shrimp for different protein options.
- Add sliced mango, papaya, or plantains to the skewers for extra tropical flair.
- Serve with coconut rice, black beans, or a side salad for a complete meal.

Per Serving: Calories: 230; Total Fat: 6g; Saturated Fat: 1g; Sodium: 780mg; Total Carbohydrates: 18g; Dietary Fiber: 2g; Total Sugars: 12g; Protein: 27g

Mahi Mahi With Cilantro-chili Butter

Ingredients:

- Salt and pepper to taste
- 4 mahi-mahi fillets
- 2 tbsp butter, melted
- 2 garlic cloves, minced
- 1/4 tsp chili powder
- 1/4 tsp lemon zest
- 1 tsp ginger, minced
- 1 tsp Worcestershire sauce
- 1 tbsp lemon juice
- 1 tbsp chopped cilantro

Directions:

1. Preheat air fryer to 190°C/375°F.
2. Combine butter, Worcestershire sauce, garlic, salt, lemon juice, ginger, pepper, lemon zest, and chili powder in a small bowl.
3. Place the mahi-mahi on a large plate, then spread the seasoned butter on the top of each.
4. Arrange the fish in a single layer in the parchment-lined frying basket. Bake for 6 minutes, then carefully flip the fish.
5. Bake for another 6-7 minutes until the fish is flaky and cooked through.
6. Serve immediately sprinkled with cilantro and enjoy.

Variations & Ingredients Tips:

- Use other firm white fish like cod or halibut.
- Add some cayenne pepper for extra heat.
- Serve over rice or with roasted vegetables.

Per Serving: Calories: 200; Total Fat: 8g; Saturated Fat: 4g; Cholesterol: 120mg; Sodium: 220mg; Total Carbs: 2g; Dietary Fiber: 0g; Total Sugars: 0g; Protein: 29g

Lemon-roasted Salmon Fillets

Cooking Time: 7 Minutes

Ingredients:

- 3 (170g) skin-on salmon fillets
- Olive oil spray
- 9 very thin lemon slices
- 3/4 teaspoon ground black pepper
- 1/4 teaspoon table salt

Directions:

1. Preheat the air fryer to 200°C/400°F.
2. Generously coat the skin of each of the fillets with olive oil spray. Set the fillets skin side down on your work surface. Place three overlapping lemon slices down the length of each salmon fillet. Sprinkle them with the pepper and salt. Coat lightly with olive oil spray.
3. Use a nonstick-safe spatula to transfer the fillets one by one to the basket, leaving as much air space between them as possible. Air-fry undisturbed for 7 minutes, or until cooked through.
4. Use a nonstick-safe spatula to transfer the fillets to serving plates. Cool for only a minute or two before serving.

Variations & Ingredients Tips:

- Use lime, orange or grapefruit slices instead of lemon.
- Sprinkle with dill, parsley or chives before air frying.
- Serve over a bed of quinoa, couscous or cauliflower rice.

Per Serving: Calories: 280; Total Fat: 16g; Saturated Fat: 3g; Cholesterol: 95mg; Sodium: 260mg; Total Carbs: 2g; Dietary Fiber: 1g; Total Sugars: 0g; Protein: 32g

Holiday Shrimp Scampi

Servings: 4 | Prep Time: 10 Minutes | Cooking Time: 25 Minutes

Ingredients:

- 680g peeled shrimp, deveined
- 1/4 tsp lemon pepper seasoning
- 6 garlic cloves, minced
- 1 tsp salt
- 1/2 tsp grated lemon zest
- 3 tbsp fresh lemon juice
- 3 tbsp sunflower oil
- 3 tbsp butter
- 2 tsp fresh thyme leaves
- 1 lemon, cut into wedges

Directions:

1. Preheat air fryer to 200°C/400°F.
2. Combine shrimp, garlic, salt and lemon pepper in a pan. Toss to coat.
3. Add lemon zest, juice, oil and butter. Mix well.
4. Place pan in air fryer basket and bake for 10-13 mins, stirring once, until shrimp is opaque.
5. Sprinkle with thyme and serve with lemon wedges.

Variations & Ingredients Tips:

- Add red pepper flakes for a kick of heat.
- Toss shrimp with parmesan before serving.
- Serve over pasta, rice or with crusty bread.

Per Serving: Calories: 285; Total Fat: 16g; Saturated Fat: 5g; Cholesterol: 285mg; Sodium: 1180mg; Total Carbs: 6g; Dietary Fiber: 1g; Total Sugars: 1g; Protein: 29g

Firecracker Popcorn Shrimp

Servings: 6 | Prep Time: 20 Minutes | Cooking Time: 8 Minutes

Ingredients:

- 1/2 cup all-purpose flour
- 2 teaspoons ground paprika
- 1 teaspoon garlic powder
- 1/2 teaspoon black pepper
- 1/4 teaspoon salt
- 2 eggs, whisked
- 1 1/2 cups panko breadcrumbs
- 450g small shrimp, peeled and deveined

Directions:

1. Preheat the air fryer to 180°C/360°F.
2. In a medium bowl, place the flour and mix in the paprika, garlic powder, pepper, and salt.

3. In a shallow dish, place the eggs.
4. In a third dish, place the breadcrumbs.
5. Assemble the shrimp by covering them in the flour, then dipping them into the egg, and then coating them with the breadcrumbs. Repeat until all the shrimp are covered in the breading.
6. Liberally spray the metal trivet that fits in the air fryer basket with olive oil mist. Place the shrimp onto the trivet, leaving space between the shrimp to flip. Cook for 4 minutes, flip the shrimp, and cook another 4 minutes. Repeat until all the shrimp are cooked.
7. Serve warm with desired dipping sauce.

Variations & Ingredients Tips:

● Add some cayenne or red pepper flakes to the flour for extra heat.
● Substitute panko with crushed tortilla chips or corn flakes.
● Serve in tacos with cabbage slaw and avocado crema.

Per Serving: Calories: 240; Total Fat: 5g; Saturated Fat: 1g; Cholesterol: 185mg; Sodium: 560mg; Total Carbs: 26g; Dietary Fiber: 1g; Total Sugars: 1g; Protein: 21g

Lemon-dill Salmon Burgers

Servings: 4 | Prep Time: 15 Minutes | Cooking Time: 8 Minutes

Ingredients:

● 2 (170g) fillets of salmon, finely chopped by hand or in a food processor
● 1 cup fine breadcrumbs
● 1 teaspoon freshly grated lemon zest
● 2 tablespoons chopped fresh dill weed
● 1 teaspoon salt
● Freshly ground black pepper
● 2 eggs, lightly beaten
● 4 brioche or hamburger buns
● Lettuce, tomato, red onion, avocado, mayonnaise or mustard, to serve

Directions:

1. Preheat the air fryer to 200°C/400°F.
2. Combine all the ingredients in a bowl. Mix together well and divide into four balls. Flatten the balls into patties, making an indentation in the center of each patty with your thumb (this will help the burger stay flat as it cooks) and flattening the sides of the burgers so that they fit nicely into the air fryer basket.
3. Transfer the burgers to the air fryer basket and air-fry for 4 minutes. Flip the burgers over and air-fry for another 3 to 4 minutes, until nicely browned and firm to the touch.
4. Serve on soft brioche buns with your choice of topping – lettuce, tomato, red onion, avocado, mayonnaise or mustard.

Variations & Ingredients Tips:

● Use canned salmon or tuna instead of fresh for convenience.
● Add some capers, olives or sun-dried tomatoes to the burger mix.
● Top with a tangy tzatziki sauce or spicy remoulade.

Per Serving: Calories: 430; Total Fat: 22g; Saturated Fat: 4.5g; Cholesterol: 170mg; Sodium: 890mg; Total Carbs: 32g; Dietary Fiber: 2g; Total Sugars: 5g; Protein: 28g

Old Bay Fish `n´ Chips

Servings: 4 | Prep Time: 20 Minutes | Cooking Time: 40 Minutes

Ingredients:

● 2 russet potatoes, peeled
● 2 tbsp olive oil
● 4 tilapia filets
● 1/4 cup flour
● Salt and pepper to taste
● 1 tsp Old Bay seasoning
● 1 lemon, zested
● 1 egg, beaten
● 1 cup panko bread crumbs
● 3 tbsp tartar sauce

Directions:

1. Preheat the air fryer to 200°C/400°F.
2. Slice the potatoes into 1.3cm-thick chips and

drizzle with olive oil. Sprinkle with salt.

3. Add the fries to the frying basket and Air Fry for 12-16 minutes, shaking once. Remove to a plate. Cover loosely with foil.
4. Sprinkle the fish with salt and season with black pepper, lemon zest, and Old Bay seasoning, then lay on a plate.
5. Put the egg in a shallow bowl and spread the panko on a separate plate.
6. Dip the fish in the flour, then the egg, then the panko. Press to coat completely.
7. Add half the fish to the frying basket and spray with cooking oil. Set a raised rack on the basket, top with the other fish, and spray with cooking oil.
8. Air Fry for 8-10 minutes until the fish flakes.
9. Serve the fish and chips with tartar sauce.

Variations & Ingredients Tips:

- Use other firm white fish like cod or haddock.
- Make sweet potato fries or wedges instead of regular potato chips.
- Serve with lemon wedges and malt vinegar on the side.

Per Serving: Calories: 375, Total Fat: 11g, Saturated Fat: 2g, Cholesterol: 130mg, Sodium: 610mg, Total Carbs: 48g, Fiber: 3g, Sugars: 2g, Protein: 21g

---

Home-style Fish Sticks

Servings: 4 | Prep Time: 15 Minutes |

Cooking Time: 30 Minutes

Ingredients:

- 450g cod fillets, cut into sticks
- 1 cup flour
- 1 egg
- 1/4 cup cornmeal
- Salt and pepper to taste
- 1/4 tsp smoked paprika
- 1 lemon

Directions:

1. Preheat air fryer at 175°C/350°F. In a bowl, add 1/2 cup of flour. In another bowl, beat the egg and in a third bowl, combine the remaining flour, cornmeal, salt, black pepper and paprika.
2. Roll the sticks in the flour, shake off excess flour. Then, dip them in the egg, shake off excess egg. Finally, dredge them in the cornmeal mixture.
3. Place fish fingers in the greased frying basket and Air Fry for 10 minutes, flipping once.
4. Serve with squeezed lemon.

Variations & Ingredients Tips:

- Use haddock, pollock or tilapia instead of cod.
- Substitute cornmeal with panko breadcrumbs for extra crunch.
- Serve with tartar sauce, ketchup or ranch dressing for dipping.

Per Serving: Calories: 260; Total Fat: 4g; Saturated Fat: 0.5g; Cholesterol: 100mg; Sodium: 200mg; Total Carbs: 29g; Dietary Fiber: 1g; Total Sugars: 0g; Protein: 28g

---

Sandwiches And Burgers Recipes

Philly Cheesesteak Sandwiches

Servings: 3 | Prep Time: 10 Minutes |

Cooking Time: 9 Minutes

Ingredients:

- 340 grams Shaved beef
- 1 tablespoon Worcestershire

sauce (gluten-free, if a concern)
- ¼ teaspoon Garlic powder
- ¼ teaspoon Mild paprika
- 6 tablespoons (45 grams) Frozen bell pepper strips (do not thaw)
- 2 slices, broken into rings Very thin yellow or white medium onion slice(s)
- 170 grams (6 to 8 slices) Provolone cheese slices
- 3 Long soft rolls such as hero, hoagie, or Italian sub rolls, or hot dog buns (gluten-free, if a concern), split open lengthwise

Directions:

1. Preheat the air fryer to 200°C/400°F.
2. When the machine is at temperature, spread the shaved beef in the basket, leaving a 1.25-cm perimeter around the meat for good air flow. Sprinkle the meat with the Worcestershire sauce, paprika, and garlic powder. Spread the peppers and onions on top of the meat.
3. Air-fry undisturbed for 6 minutes, or until cooked through. Set the cheese on top of the meat. Continue air-frying undisturbed for 3 minutes, or until the cheese has melted.
4. Use kitchen tongs to divide the meat and cheese layers in the basket between the rolls or buns. Serve hot.

Variations & Ingredients Tips:

- Use thinly sliced ribeye or sirloin steak instead of shaved beef for a more traditional texture.
- Add sliced mushrooms to the pepper and onion mixture for extra flavor and nutrition.
- Substitute provolone with American cheese or Cheez Whiz for a classic Philly taste.

Per Serving: Calories: 620; Cholesterol: 135mg; Total Fat: 32g; Saturated Fat: 15g; Sodium: 1320mg; Total Carbohydrates: 38g; Dietary Fiber: 2g; Total Sugars: 5g; Protein: 48g

Chicken Gyros

Servings: 4 | Prep Time: 10 Minutes (plus Marinating Time) | Cooking Time: 14 Minutes

Ingredients:

- 4 110to 140-gram boneless skinless chicken thighs, trimmed of any fat blobs
- 2 tablespoons Lemon juice
- 2 tablespoons Red wine vinegar
- 2 tablespoons Olive oil
- 2 teaspoons Dried oregano
- 2 teaspoons Minced garlic
- 1 teaspoon Table salt
- 1 teaspoon Ground black pepper
- 4 Pita pockets (gluten-free, if a concern)
- ½ cup Chopped tomatoes
- ½ cup Bottled regular, low-fat, or fat-free ranch dressing (gluten-free, if a concern)

Directions:

1. Mix the thighs, lemon juice, vinegar, oil, oregano, garlic, salt, and pepper in a zip-closed bag. Seal, gently massage the marinade into the meat through the plastic, and refrigerate for at least 2 hours or up to 6 hours. (Longer than that and the meat can turn rubbery.)
2. Set the plastic bag out on the counter (to make the contents a little less frigid). Preheat the air fryer to 190°C/375°F.
3. When the machine is at temperature, use kitchen tongs to place the thighs in the basket in one layer. Discard the marinade. Air-fry the chicken thighs undisturbed for 12 minutes, or until browned and an instant-read meat thermometer inserted into the thickest part of one thigh registers 75°C/165°F. You may need to air-fry the chicken 2 minutes longer if the machine's temperature is 70°C/360°F.
4. Use kitchen tongs to transfer the thighs to a cutting board. Cool for 5 minutes, then set one thigh in each of the pita pockets. Top each with 2 tablespoons chopped tomatoes and 2 tablespoons dressing. Serve warm.

Variations & Ingredients Tips:

- Substitute chicken thighs with chicken breast for a leaner option.
- Add shredded lettuce, sliced onions, or

cucumbers for extra crunch and flavor.

- Use homemade tzatziki sauce instead of ranch dressing for a more authentic taste.

Per Serving: Calories: 460; Cholesterol: 95mg; Total Fat: 28g; Saturated Fat: 5g; Sodium: 1070mg; Total Carbohydrates: 29g; Dietary Fiber: 2g; Total Sugars: 4g; Protein: 25g

Chili Cheese Dogs

Servings: 3 | Prep Time: 10 Minutes | Cooking Time: 12 Minutes

Ingredients:

- 340 grams Lean ground beef
- 1½ tablespoons Chile powder
- 240 grams plus 2 tablespoons Jarred sofrito
- 3 Hot dogs (gluten-free, if a con-
- cern)
- 3 Hot dog buns (gluten-free, if a concern), split open lengthwise
- 3 tablespoons Finely chopped scallion
- 60 grams Shredded Cheddar cheese

Directions:

1. Crumble the ground beef into a medium or large saucepan set over medium heat. Brown well, stirring often to break up the clumps. Add the chile powder and cook for 30 seconds, stirring the whole time. Stir in the sofrito and bring to a simmer. Reduce the heat to low and simmer, stirring occasionally, for 5 minutes. Keep warm.
2. Preheat the air fryer to 200°C/400°F.
3. When the machine is at temperature, put the hot dogs in the basket and air-fry undisturbed for 10 minutes, or until the hot dogs are bubbling and blistered, even a little crisp.
4. Use kitchen tongs to put the hot dogs in the buns. Top each with about 120 grams of the ground beef mixture, 1 tablespoon of the minced scallion, and 20 grams of the cheese. (The scallion should go under the cheese so it superheats and wilts a bit.) Set the filled hot dog buns in the basket and air-fry undisturbed for 2 minutes, or until the cheese has melted.

5. Remove the basket from the machine. Cool the chili cheese dogs in the basket for 5 minutes before serving.

Variations & Ingredients Tips:

- Use turkey or veggie hot dogs for a healthier option.
- Substitute cheddar cheese with your favorite melty cheese, such as pepper jack or Swiss.
- Add diced onions or jalapeños to the chili for extra flavor and heat.

Per Serving: Calories: 580; Cholesterol: 110mg; Total Fat: 32g; Saturated Fat: 13g; Sodium: 1420mg; Total Carbohydrates: 36g; Dietary Fiber: 5g; Total Sugars: 6g; Protein: 38g

Inside Out Cheeseburgers

Servings: 2 | Prep Time: 15 Minutes | Cooking Time: 20 Minutes

Ingredients:

- 340 grams lean ground beef
- 3 tablespoons minced onion
- 4 teaspoons ketchup
- 2 teaspoons yellow mustard
- salt and freshly
- ground black pepper
- 4 slices of Cheddar cheese, broken into smaller pieces
- 8 hamburger dill pickle chips

Directions:

1. Combine the ground beef, minced onion, ketchup, mustard, salt and pepper in a large bowl. Mix well to thoroughly combine the ingredients. Divide the meat into four equal portions.
2. To make the stuffed burgers, flatten each portion of meat into a thin patty. Place 4 pickle chips and half of the cheese onto the center of two of the patties, leaving a rim around the edge of the patty exposed. Place the remaining two patties on top of the first and press the meat together firmly, sealing the edges tightly. With the burgers on a flat surface, press the sides of the burger with the palm of your hand to create

a straight edge. This will help keep the stuffing inside the burger while it cooks.
3. Preheat the air fryer to 190°C/370°F.
4. Place the burgers inside the air fryer basket and air-fry for 20 minutes, flipping the burgers over halfway through the cooking time.
5. Serve the cheeseburgers on buns with lettuce and tomato.

Variations & Ingredients Tips:

● Use different types of cheese like Swiss, pepper jack, or blue cheese for a unique flavor.
● Add crispy bacon pieces or sautéed mushrooms to the stuffing for extra richness.
● Brush the burgers with a mixture of melted butter and minced garlic before cooking for added flavor.

Per Serving (1 burger): Calories: 510; Cholesterol: 145mg; Total Fat: 32g; Saturated Fat: 14g; Sodium: 780mg; Total Carbohydrates: 12g; Dietary Fiber: 1g; Total Sugars: 6g; Protein: 42g

Chicken Apple Brie Melt

Servings: 3 | Prep Time: 10 Minutes | Cooking Time: 13 Minutes

Ingredients:

● 3 140 to 170-gram boneless skinless chicken breasts
● Vegetable oil spray
● 1½ teaspoons Dried herbes de Provence
● 85 grams Brie, rind removed, thinly sliced
● 6 Thin cored apple slices
● 3 French rolls (gluten-free, if a concern)
● 2 tablespoons Dijon mustard (gluten-free, if a concern)

Directions:

1. Preheat the air fryer to 190°C/375°F .
2. Lightly coat all sides of the chicken breasts with vegetable oil spray. Sprinkle the breasts evenly with the herbes de Provence.
3. When the machine is at temperature, set the breasts in the basket and air-fry undisturbed for 10 minutes.
4. Top the chicken breasts with the apple slices, then the cheese. Air-fry undisturbed for 2 minutes, or until the cheese is melty and bubbling.
5. Use a nonstick-safe spatula and kitchen tongs, for balance, to transfer the breasts to a cutting board. Set the rolls in the basket and air-fry for 1 minute to warm through. (Putting them in the machine without splitting them keeps the insides very soft while the outside gets a little crunchy.)
6. Transfer the rolls to the cutting board. Split them open lengthwise, then spread 1 teaspoon mustard on each cut side. Set a prepared chicken breast on the bottom of a roll and close with its top, repeating as necessary to make additional sandwiches. Serve warm.

Variations & Ingredients Tips:

● Substitute the Brie with Camembert or another soft cheese of your choice.
● Use pears instead of apples for a different flavor profile.
● Add baby spinach or arugula for extra greens and nutrition.

Per Serving: Calories: 510; Cholesterol: 135mg; Total Fat: 19g; Saturated Fat: 8g; Sodium: 670mg; Total Carbohydrates: 41g; Dietary Fiber: 2g; Total Sugars: 6g; Protein: 45g

Sausage And Pepper Heros

Servings: 3 | Prep Time: 10 Minutes | Cooking Time: 11 Minutes

Ingredients:

● 3 links (about 255 grams total) Sweet Italian sausages (gluten-free, if a concern)
● 1½ Medium red or green bell pepper(s), stemmed, cored, and cut into 1.25-cm-wide strips
● 1 medium Yellow or white onion(s), peeled, halved, and sliced into thin half-moons
● 3 Long soft rolls, such as hero, hoagie, or Italian sub rolls (gluten-free, if a concern), split

open lengthwise

For garnishing Balsamic vinegar

For garnishing Fresh basil leaves

Directions:

1. Preheat the air fryer to 200°C/400°F.
2. When the machine is at temperature, set the sausage links in the basket in one layer and air-fry undisturbed for 5 minutes.
3. Add the pepper strips and onions. Continue air-frying, tossing and rearranging everything about once every minute, for 5 minutes, or until the sausages are browned and an instant-read meat thermometer inserted into one of the links registers 70°C/160°F.
4. Use a nonstick-safe spatula and kitchen tongs to transfer the sausages and vegetables to a cutting board. Set the rolls cut side down in the basket in one layer (working in batches as necessary) and air-fry undisturbed for 1 minute, to toast the rolls a bit and warm them up. Set 1 sausage with some pepper strips and onions in each warm roll, sprinkle balsamic vinegar over the sandwich fillings, and garnish with basil leaves.

Variations & Ingredients Tips:

- Use hot Italian sausage or chorizo for a spicier sandwich.
- Add sliced mushrooms or zucchini to the pepper and onion mixture for extra veggies.
- Top with shredded mozzarella or provolone cheese for a cheesy twist.

Per Serving (1 sandwich): Calories: 560; Cholesterol: 60mg; Total Fat: 36g; Saturated Fat: 12g; Sodium: 1420mg; Total Carbohydrates: 39g; Dietary Fiber: 3g; Total Sugars: 7g; Protein: 24g

---

Thanksgiving Turkey Sandwiches

Servings: 3 | Prep Time: 15 Minutes | Cooking Time: 10 Minutes

Ingredients:

- 1½ cups Herb-seasoned stuffing mix (not cornbread-style; gluten-free, if a concern)
- 1 Large egg white(s)
- 2 tablespoons Water
- 3 140- to 170-gram turkey breast cutlets
- Vegetable oil spray
- 4½ tablespoons Purchased cranberry sauce, preferably whole berry
- ⅛ teaspoon Ground cinnamon
- ⅛ teaspoon Ground dried ginger
- 4½ tablespoons Regular, low-fat, or fat-free mayonnaise (gluten-free, if a concern)
- 6 tablespoons Shredded Brussels sprouts
- 3 Kaiser rolls (gluten-free, if a concern), split open

Directions:

1. Preheat the air fryer to 190°C/375°F.
2. Put the stuffing mix in a heavy zip-closed bag, seal it, lay it flat on your counter, and roll a rolling pin over the bag to crush the stuffing mix to the consistency of rough sand. (Or you can pulse the stuffing mix to the desired consistency in a food processor.)
3. Set up and fill two shallow soup plates or small pie plates on your counter: one for the egg white(s), whisked with the water until foamy; and one for the ground stuffing mix.
4. Dip a cutlet in the egg white mixture, coating both sides and letting any excess egg white slip back into the rest. Set the cutlet in the ground stuffing mix and coat it evenly on both sides, pressing gently to coat well on both sides. Lightly coat the cutlet on both sides with vegetable oil spray, set it aside, and continue dipping and coating the remaining cutlets in the same way.
5. Set the cutlets in the basket and air-fry undisturbed for 10 minutes, or until crisp and brown. Use kitchen tongs to transfer the cutlets to a wire rack to cool for a few minutes.
6. Meanwhile, stir the cranberry sauce with the cinnamon and ginger in a small bowl. Mix the shredded Brussels sprouts and mayonnaise in a second bowl until the vegetable is evenly coated.
7. Build the sandwiches by spreading about 1½

tablespoons of the cranberry mixture on the cut side of the bottom half of each roll. Set a cutlet on top, then spread about 3 tablespoons of the Brussels sprouts mixture evenly over the cutlet. Set the other half of the roll on top and serve warm.

Variations & Ingredients Tips:

● Use leftover roasted turkey instead of turkey cutlets for a post-Thanksgiving sandwich.
● Substitute Brussels sprouts with shredded cabbage or kale for a different texture and flavor.
● Add a slice of brie or provolone cheese to the sandwich for extra creaminess.

Per Serving: Calories: 530; Cholesterol: 75mg; Total Fat: 22g; Saturated Fat: 4g; Sodium: 1180mg; Total Carbohydrates: 53g; Dietary Fiber: 4g; Total Sugars: 15g; Protein: 33g

White Bean Veggie Burgers

Servings: 3 | Prep Time: 15 Minutes | Cooking Time: 13 Minutes

Ingredients:

● 320 grams Drained and rinsed canned white beans
● 3 tablespoons Rolled oats (not quick-cooking or steel-cut; gluten-free, if a concern)
● 3 tablespoons Chopped walnuts
● 2 teaspoons Olive oil
● 2 teaspoons Lemon juice
● 1½ teaspoons Dijon mustard (gluten-free, if a concern)
● ¾ teaspoon Dried sage leaves
● ¼ teaspoon Table salt
● Olive oil spray
● 3 Whole-wheat buns or gluten-free whole-grain buns (if a concern), split open

Directions:

1. Preheat the air fryer to 200°C/400°F.
2. Place the beans, oats, walnuts, oil, lemon juice,

mustard, sage, and salt in a food processor. Cover and process to make a coarse paste that will hold its shape, about like wet sugar-cookie dough, stopping the machine to scrape down the inside of the canister at least once.
3. Scrape down and remove the blade. With clean and wet hands, form the bean paste into two 10-cm patties for the small batch, three 10-cm patties for the medium, or four 10-cm patties for the large batch. Generously coat the patties on both sides with olive oil spray.
4. Set them in the basket with some space between them and air-fry undisturbed for 12 minutes, or until lightly brown and crisp at the edges. The tops of the burgers will feel firm to the touch.
5. Use a nonstick-safe spatula, and perhaps a flatware fork for balance, to transfer the burgers to a cutting board. Set the buns cut side down in the basket in one layer (working in batches as necessary) and air-fry undisturbed for 1 minute, to toast a bit and warm up. Serve the burgers warm in the buns.

Variations & Ingredients Tips:

● Use black beans, chickpeas, or lentils instead of white beans for a different flavor and color.
● Add grated carrots, zucchini, or beets to the burger mixture for extra nutrition and texture.
● Serve with your favorite burger toppings like lettuce, tomato, onion, and pickles.

Per Serving (1 burger): Calories: 350; Cholesterol: 0mg; Total Fat: 13g; Saturated Fat: 1g; Sodium: 520mg; Total Carbohydrates: 48g; Dietary Fiber: 9g; Total Sugars: 4g; Protein: 14g

Salmon Burgers

Servings: 3 | Prep Time: 15 Minutes | Cooking Time: 8 Minutes

Ingredients:

● 510 grams Skinless salmon fillet, preferably fattier Atlantic salmon
● 1½ tablespoons
Minced chives or the green part of a scallion
● ½ cup Plain panko bread crumbs (glu-

ten-free, if a concern)
- 1½ teaspoons Dijon mustard (gluten-free, if a concern)
- 1½ teaspoons Drained and rinsed capers, minced
- 1½ teaspoons Lemon juice
- ¼ teaspoon Table salt
- ¼ teaspoon Ground black pepper
- Vegetable oil spray

Directions:

1. Preheat the air fryer to 190°C/375°F.
2. Cut the salmon into pieces that will fit in a food processor. Cover and pulse until coarsely chopped. Add the chives and pulse to combine, until the fish is ground but not a paste. Scrape down and remove the blade. Scrape the salmon mixture into a bowl. Add the bread crumbs, mustard, capers, lemon juice, salt, and pepper. Stir gently until well combined.
3. Use clean and dry hands to form the mixture into two 12.5-cm patties for a small batch, three 12.5-cm patties for a medium batch, or four 12.5-cm patties for a large one.
4. Coat both sides of each patty with vegetable oil spray. Set them in the basket in one layer and air-fry undisturbed for 8 minutes, or until browned and an instant-read meat thermometer inserted into the center of a burger registers 65°C/145°F.
5. Use a nonstick-safe spatula, and perhaps a flatware fork for balance, to transfer the burgers to a wire rack. Cool for 2 or 3 minutes before serving.

Variations & Ingredients Tips:

- Substitute salmon with canned or leftover cooked salmon for convenience.
- Add finely chopped red bell pepper or celery to the burger mixture for extra crunch and flavor.
- Serve on toasted buns with lettuce, tomato, and a dollop of tartar sauce or remoulade.

Per Serving (1 burger): Calories: 320; Cholesterol: 95mg; Total Fat: 16g; Saturated Fat: 3g; Sodium: 440mg; Total Carbohydrates: 15g; Dietary Fiber: 1g; Total Sugars: 1g; Protein: 31g

Eggplant Parmesan Subs

Servings: 2 | Prep Time: 10 Minutes | Cooking Time: 13 Minutes

Ingredients:

- 4 Peeled eggplant slices (about 1.25 cm thick and 7.5 cm in diameter)
- Olive oil spray
- 2 tablespoons plus 2 teaspoons Jarred pizza sauce, any variety except creamy
- ¼ cup (about 20 grams) Finely grated Parmesan cheese
- 2 Small, long soft rolls, such as hero, hoagie, or Italian sub rolls (gluten-free, if a concern), split open lengthwise

Directions:

1. Preheat the air fryer to 175°C/350°F.
2. When the machine is at temperature, coat both sides of the eggplant slices with olive oil spray. Set them in the basket in one layer and air-fry undisturbed for 10 minutes, until lightly browned and softened.
3. Increase the machine's temperature to 190°C/375°F (or 185°C/370°F, if that's the closest setting—unless the machine is already at 180°C/360°F, in which case leave it alone). Top each eggplant slice with 2 teaspoons pizza sauce, then 1 tablespoon of cheese. Air-fry undisturbed for 2 minutes, or until the cheese has melted.
4. Use a nonstick-safe spatula, and perhaps a flatware fork for balance, to transfer the eggplant slices cheese side up to a cutting board. Set the roll(s) cut side down in the basket in one layer (working in batches as necessary) and air-fry undisturbed for 1 minute, to toast the rolls a bit and warm them up. Set 2 eggplant slices in each warm roll.

Variations & Ingredients Tips:

- Use zucchini slices instead of eggplant for a different vegetable option.
- Add a slice of fresh mozzarella on top of the Parmesan for extra cheesiness.

- Sprinkle some dried herbs like oregano or basil on the eggplant before cooking for extra flavor.

Per Serving (1 sandwich): Calories: 280; Cholesterol: 10mg; Total Fat: 9g; Saturated Fat: 3g; Sodium: 840mg; Total Carbohydrates: 40g; Dietary Fiber: 5g; Total Sugars: 8g; Protein: 11g

Perfect Burgers

Servings: 3 | Prep Time: 10 Minutes | Cooking Time: 13 Minutes

Ingredients:

- 510 grams 90% lean ground beef
- 1½ tablespoons Worcestershire sauce (gluten-free, if a concern)
- ½ teaspoon Ground black pepper
- 3 Hamburger buns (gluten-free if a concern), split open

Directions:

1. Preheat the air fryer to 190°C/375°F.
2. Gently mix the ground beef, Worcestershire sauce, and pepper in a bowl until well combined but preserving as much of the meat's fibers as possible. Divide this mixture into two 15-cm patties for the small batch, three 12.5-cm patties for the medium, or four 12.5-cm patties for the large. Make a thumbprint indentation in the center of each patty, about halfway through the meat.
3. Set the patties in the basket in one layer with some space between them. Air-fry undisturbed for 10 minutes, or until an instant-read meat thermometer inserted into the center of a burger registers 70°C/160°F (a medium-well burger). You may need to add 2 minutes cooking time if the air fryer is at 180°C/360°F.
4. Use a nonstick-safe spatula, and perhaps a flatware fork for balance, to transfer the burgers to a cutting board. Set the buns cut side down in the basket in one layer (working in batches as necessary) and air-fry undisturbed for 1 minute, to toast a bit and warm up. Serve the burgers in the warm buns.

Variations & Ingredients Tips:

- Mix in finely chopped onions, garlic, or herbs to the burger mixture for extra flavor.
- Use a mixture of ground beef and ground pork or lamb for a juicier, more flavorful burger.
- Top burgers with your favorite cheese, bacon, avocado, or sautéed mushrooms.

Per Serving (1 burger): Calories: 420; Cholesterol: 105mg; Total Fat: 22g; Saturated Fat: 8g; Sodium: 460mg; Total Carbohydrates: 23g; Dietary Fiber: 1g; Total Sugars: 3g; Protein: 34g

Chicken Saltimbocca Sandwiches

Servings: 3 | Prep Time: 10 Minutes | Cooking Time: 11 Minutes

Ingredients:

- 3 140to 170-gram boneless skinless chicken breasts
- 6 Thin prosciutto slices
- 6 Provolone cheese slices
- 3 Long soft rolls, such as hero, hoagie, or Italian sub rolls (gluten-free, if a concern), split open lengthwise
- 3 tablespoons Pesto, purchased or homemade (see the headnote)

Directions:

1. Preheat the air fryer to 200°C/400°F.
2. Wrap each chicken breast with 2 prosciutto slices, spiraling the prosciutto around the breast and overlapping the slices a bit to cover the breast. The prosciutto will stick to the chicken more readily than bacon does.
3. When the machine is at temperature, set the wrapped chicken breasts in the basket and air-fry undisturbed for 10 minutes, or until the prosciutto is frizzled and the chicken is cooked through.
4. Overlap 2 cheese slices on each breast. Air-fry undisturbed for 1 minute, or until melted. Take the basket out of the machine.

5. Smear the insides of the rolls with the pesto, then use kitchen tongs to put a wrapped and cheesy chicken breast in each roll.

Variations & Ingredients Tips:

- Use fresh mozzarella instead of provolone for a creamier texture.
- Add sliced tomatoes or roasted red peppers for extra flavor and nutrition.
- Substitute prosciutto with ham or bacon if desired.

Per Serving: Calories: 630; Cholesterol: 125mg; Total Fat: 32g; Saturated Fat: 11g; Sodium: 1580mg; Total Carbohydrates: 38g; Dietary Fiber: 2g; Total Sugars: 4g; Protein: 48g

Provolone Stuffed Meatballs

Servings: 4 | Prep Time: 20 Minutes | Cooking Time: 12 Minutes

Ingredients:

- 1 tablespoon olive oil
- 1 small onion, very finely chopped
- 1 to 2 cloves garlic, minced
- 340 grams ground beef
- 340 grams ground pork
- ¾ cup breadcrumbs
- ¼ cup grated Parmesan cheese
- ¼ cup finely
- chopped fresh parsley (or 1 tablespoon dried parsley)
- ½ teaspoon dried oregano
- 1½ teaspoons salt
- freshly ground black pepper
- 2 eggs, lightly beaten
- 140 grams sharp or aged provolone cheese, cut into 2.5-cm cubes

Directions:

1. Preheat a skillet over medium-high heat. Add the oil and cook the onion and garlic until tender, but not browned.
2. Transfer the onion and garlic to a large bowl and add the beef, pork, breadcrumbs, Parmesan cheese, parsley, oregano, salt, pepper and eggs. Mix well until all the ingredients are combined.

Divide the mixture into 12 evenly sized balls. Make one meatball at a time, by pressing a hole in the meatball mixture with your finger and pushing a piece of provolone cheese into the hole. Mold the meat back into a ball, enclosing the cheese.

3. Preheat the air fryer to 190°C/380°F.
4. Working in two batches, transfer six of the meatballs to the air fryer basket and air-fry for 12 minutes, shaking the basket and turning the meatballs a couple of times during the cooking process. Repeat with the remaining six meatballs. You can pop the first batch of meatballs into the air fryer for the last two minutes of cooking to re-heat them. Serve warm.

Variations & Ingredients Tips:

- Substitute beef and pork with ground turkey or chicken for a leaner meatball option.
- Use mozzarella or fontina cheese instead of provolone for a milder flavor.
- Serve meatballs with marinara sauce, in sub rolls, or over pasta for a complete meal.

Per Serving (3 meatballs): Calories: 520; Cholesterol: 180mg; Total Fat: 36g; Saturated Fat: 15g; Sodium: 1160mg; Total Carbohydrates: 18g; Dietary Fiber: 1g; Total Sugars: 2g; Protein: 35g

Lamb Burgers

Servings: 3 | Prep Time: 15 Minutes | Cooking Time: 17 Minutes

Ingredients:

- 510 grams Ground lamb
- 3 tablespoons Crumbled feta
- 1 teaspoon Minced garlic
- 1 teaspoon Tomato paste
- ¾ teaspoon Ground coriander
- ¾ teaspoon Ground dried ginger
- Up to ⅛ teaspoon Cayenne
- Up to a ⅛ teaspoon Table salt (optional)
- 3 Kaiser rolls or hamburger buns (gluten-free, if a concern), split open

Directions:

1. Preheat the air fryer to 190°C/375°F.
2. Gently mix the ground lamb, feta, garlic, tomato paste, coriander, ginger, cayenne, and salt (if using) in a bowl until well combined, trying to keep the bits of cheese intact. Form this mixture into two 15-cm patties for the small batch, three 12.5-cm patties for the medium, or four 12.5-cm patties for the large.
3. Set the patties in the basket in one layer and air-fry undisturbed for 16 minutes, or until an instant-read meat thermometer inserted into one burger registers 70°C/160°F. (The cheese is not an issue with the temperature probe in this recipe as it was for the Inside-Out Cheeseburgers, because the feta is so well mixed into the ground meat.)
4. Use a nonstick-safe spatula, and perhaps a flatware fork for balance, to transfer the burgers to a cutting board. Set the buns cut side down in the basket in one layer (working in batches as necessary) and air-fry undisturbed for 1 minute, to toast a bit and warm up. Serve the burgers warm in the buns.

Variations & Ingredients Tips:

- Substitute feta with goat cheese or crumbled blue cheese for a different flavor profile.
- Add finely chopped mint or parsley to the lamb mixture for a fresh, herbal taste.
- Serve with tzatziki sauce, sliced cucumbers, and red onions for a Greek-inspired burger.

Per Serving (1 burger): Calories: 560; Cholesterol: 140mg; Total Fat: 34g; Saturated Fat: 15g; Sodium: 580mg; Total Carbohydrates: 25g; Dietary Fiber: 1g; Total Sugars: 3g; Protein: 38g

Reuben Sandwiches

Servings: 2 | Prep Time: 10 Minutes | Cooking Time: 11 Minutes

Ingredients:

- 225 grams Sliced deli corned beef
- 4 teaspoons Regular or low-fat mayonnaise (not fat-free)
- 4 Rye bread slices
- 2 tablespoons plus 2 teaspoons Russian dressing
- ½ cup Purchased sauerkraut, squeezed by the handful over the sink to get rid of excess moisture
- 55 grams (2 to 4 slices) Swiss cheese slices (optional)

Directions:

1. Set the corned beef in the basket, slip the basket into the machine, and heat the air fryer to 200°C/400°F. Air-fry undisturbed for 3 minutes from the time the basket is put in the machine, just to warm up the meat.
2. Use kitchen tongs to transfer the corned beef to a cutting board. Spread 1 teaspoon mayonnaise on one side of each slice of rye bread, rubbing the mayonnaise into the bread with a small flatware knife.
3. Place the bread slices mayonnaise side down on a cutting board. Spread the Russian dressing over the "dry" side of each slice. For one sandwich, top one slice of bread with the corned beef, sauerkraut, and cheese (if using). For two sandwiches, top two slices of bread each with half of the corned beef, sauerkraut, and cheese (if using). Close the sandwiches with the remaining bread, setting it mayonnaise side up on top.
4. Set the sandwich(es) in the basket and air-fry undisturbed for 8 minutes, or until browned and crunchy.
5. Use a nonstick-safe spatula, and perhaps a flatware fork for balance, to transfer the sandwich(es) to a cutting board. Cool for 2 or 3 minutes before slicing in half and serving.

Variations & Ingredients Tips:

- Substitute corned beef with pastrami for a classic New York deli taste.
- Use Thousand Island dressing instead of Russian dressing for a tangy, sweet flavor.
- Add sliced dill pickles or mustard to the sandwich for extra zing.

Per Serving (1 sandwich): Calories: 520; Cholesterol: 75mg; Total Fat: 30g; Saturated Fat: 9g; Sodium: 2020mg; Total Carbohydrates: 36g; Dietary Fiber: 4g; Total Sugars: 6g; Protein: 29g

Chicken Club Sandwiches

Servings: 3 | Prep Time: 15 Minutes | Cooking Time: 15 Minutes

Ingredients:

- 3 140- to 170-gram boneless skinless chicken breasts
- 6 Thick-cut bacon strips (gluten-free, if a concern)
- 3 Long soft rolls, such as hero, hoagie, or Italian sub rolls (gluten-free, if a concern)
- 3 tablespoons Regular, low-fat, or fat-free mayonnaise (gluten-free, if a concern)
- 3 Lettuce leaves, preferably romaine or iceberg
- 6 6-mm-thick tomato slices

Directions:

1. Preheat the air fryer to 190°C/375°F.
2. Wrap each chicken breast with 2 strips of bacon, spiraling the bacon around the meat, slightly overlapping the strips on each revolution. Start the second strip of bacon farther down the breast but on a line with the start of the first strip so they both end at a lined-up point on the chicken breast.
3. When the machine is at temperature, set the wrapped breasts bacon-seam side down in the basket with space between them. Air-fry undisturbed for 12 minutes, until the bacon is browned, crisp, and cooked through and an instant-read meat thermometer inserted into the center of a breast registers 75°C/165°F. You may need to add 2 minutes in the air fryer if the temperature is at 70°C/160°F.
4. Use kitchen tongs to transfer the breasts to a wire rack. Split the rolls open lengthwise and set them cut side down in the basket. Air-fry for 1 minute, or until warmed through.
5. Use kitchen tongs to transfer the rolls to a cutting board. Spread 1 tablespoon mayonnaise on the cut side of one half of each roll. Top with a chicken breast, lettuce leaf, and tomato slice. Serve warm.

Variations & Ingredients Tips:

- Use turkey bacon for a lower-fat option.
- Add sliced avocado or pickled onions for extra flavor and texture.
- Toast the rolls before assembling the sandwiches for a crispy texture.

Per Serving: Calories: 640; Cholesterol: 110mg; Total Fat: 34g; Saturated Fat: 9g; Sodium: 1180mg; Total Carbohydrates: 44g; Dietary Fiber: 2g; Total Sugars: 5g; Protein: 42g

Crunchy Falafel Balls

Servings: 8 | Prep Time: 15 Minutes | Cooking Time: 16 Minutes

Ingredients:

- 600 grams Drained and rinsed canned chickpeas
- 60 grams Olive oil
- 3 tablespoons All-purpose flour
- 1½ teaspoons Dried oregano
- 1½ teaspoons Dried sage leaves
- 1½ teaspoons Dried thyme
- ¾ teaspoon Table salt
- Olive oil spray

Directions:

1. Preheat the air fryer to 200°C/400°F.
2. Place the chickpeas, olive oil, flour, oregano, sage, thyme, and salt in a food processor. Cover and process into a paste, stopping the machine at least once to scrape down the inside of the canister.
3. Scrape down and remove the blade. Using clean, wet hands, form 2 tablespoons of the paste into a ball, then continue making 9 more balls for a small batch, 15 more for a medium one, and 19 more for a large batch. Generously coat the balls in olive oil spray.
4. Set the balls in the basket in one layer with a little space between them and air-fry undisturbed for 16 minutes, or until well browned and crisp.
5. Dump the contents of the basket onto a wire rack. Cool for 5 minutes before serving.

Variations & Ingredients Tips:

- Add minced garlic, onion, or herbs like parsley or cilantro for extra flavor.
- Serve with tahini sauce, hummus, or tzatziki for dipping.
- Make a falafel sandwich by stuffing pita bread with falafel balls, lettuce, tomato, and sauce.

Per Serving (2 falafel balls): Calories: 170; Cholesterol: 0mg; Total Fat: 9g; Saturated Fat: 1g; Sodium: 230mg; Total Carbohydrates: 18g; Dietary Fiber: 4g; Total Sugars: 2g; Protein: 5g

Asian Glazed Meatballs

Servings: 4 | Prep Time: 15 Minutes | Cooking Time: 10 Minutes

Ingredients:

- 1 large shallot, finely chopped
- 2 cloves garlic, minced
- 1 tablespoon grated fresh ginger
- 2 teaspoons fresh thyme, finely chopped
- 1½ cups brown mushrooms, very finely chopped (a food processor works well here)
- 2 tablespoons soy sauce
- freshly ground black pepper
- ½ kg ground beef
- ¼ kg ground pork
- 3 egg yolks
- 1 cup Thai sweet chili sauce (spring roll sauce)
- ¼ cup toasted sesame seeds
- 2 scallions, sliced

Directions:

1. Combine the shallot, garlic, ginger, thyme, mushrooms, soy sauce, freshly ground black pepper, ground beef and pork, and egg yolks in a bowl and mix the ingredients together. Gently shape the mixture into 24 balls, about the size of a golf ball.
2. Preheat the air fryer to 190°C/380°F.
3. Working in batches, air-fry the meatballs for 8 minutes, turning the meatballs over halfway through the cooking time. Drizzle some of the Thai sweet chili sauce on top of each meatball and return the basket to the air fryer, air-frying for another 2 minutes. Reserve the remaining

Thai sweet chili sauce for serving.
4. As soon as the meatballs are done, sprinkle with toasted sesame seeds and transfer them to a serving platter. Scatter the scallions around and serve warm.

Variations & Ingredients Tips:

- Use a food processor to finely chop the mushrooms for better texture in the meatballs.
- Work in batches when air frying the meatballs to ensure even cooking and browning.
- Drizzle the Thai sweet chili sauce over the meatballs towards the end of cooking for a nice glaze.

Per Serving: Calories: 550; Cholesterol: 205mg; Total Fat: 32g; Saturated Fat: 11g; Sodium: 1300mg; Total Carbohydrates: 36g; Dietary Fiber: 2g; Total Sugars: 23g; Protein: 29g

Thai-style Pork Sliders

Servings: 4 | Prep Time: 15 Minutes | Cooking Time: 15 Minutes

Ingredients:

- 310 grams Ground pork
- 2½ tablespoons Very thinly sliced scallions, white and green parts
- 4 teaspoons Minced peeled fresh ginger
- 2½ teaspoons Fish sauce (gluten-free, if a concern)
- 2 teaspoons Thai
- curry paste (see the headnote; gluten-free, if a concern)
- 2 teaspoons Light brown sugar
- ¾ teaspoon Ground black pepper
- 4 Slider buns (gluten-free, if a concern)

Directions:

1. Preheat the air fryer to 190°C/375°F.
2. Gently mix the pork, scallions, ginger, fish sauce, curry paste, brown sugar, and black pepper in a bowl until well combined. With clean, wet hands, form about 80 grams of the pork mixture into a slider about 6.5-cm in diameter.

Repeat until you use up all the meat—3 sliders for the small batch, 4 for the medium, and 6 for the large. (Keep wetting your hands to help the patties adhere.)

3. When the machine is at temperature, set the sliders in the basket in one layer. Air-fry undisturbed for 14 minutes, or until the sliders are golden brown and caramelized at their edges and an instant-read meat thermometer inserted into the center of a slider registers 70°C/160°F.

4. Use a nonstick-safe spatula, and perhaps a flat-ware fork for balance, to transfer the sliders to a cutting board. Set the buns cut side down in the basket in one layer (working in batches as necessary) and air-fry undisturbed for 1 minute, to toast a bit and warm up. Serve the sliders warm in the buns.

Variations & Ingredients Tips:

- Use ground chicken or turkey for a leaner slider option.
- Substitute Thai curry paste with red curry paste or green curry paste for a different flavor profile.
- Serve with pickled vegetables, cilantro, and sriracha mayonnaise for extra Thai-inspired toppings.

Per Serving (1 slider): Calories: 240; Cholesterol: 65mg; Total Fat: 13g; Saturated Fat: 4g; Sodium: 490mg; Total Carbohydrates: 18g; Dietary Fiber: 1g; Total Sugars: 4g; Protein: 15g

Black Bean Veggie Burgers

Servings: 3 | Prep Time: 15 Minutes | Cooking Time: 10 Minutes

Ingredients:

- 1 cup Drained and rinsed canned black beans
- ⅓ cup Pecan pieces
- ⅓ cup Rolled oats (not quick-cooking or steel-cut; gluten-free, if a concern)
- 2 tablespoons (or 1 small egg) Pasteurized egg substitute, such as Egg Beaters (gluten-free, if a concern)
- 2 teaspoons Red ketchup-like chili sauce, such as Heinz
- ¼ teaspoon Ground cumin
- ¼ teaspoon Dried oregano
- ¼ teaspoon Table salt
- ¼ teaspoon Ground black pepper
- Olive oil
- Olive oil spray

Directions:

1. Preheat the air fryer to 200°C/400°F.
2. Put the beans, pecans, oats, egg substitute or egg, chili sauce, cumin, oregano, salt, and pepper in a food processor. Cover and process to a coarse paste that will hold its shape like sugar-cookie dough, adding olive oil in 1-teaspoon increments to get the mixture to blend smoothly. The amount of olive oil is actually dependent on the internal moisture content of the beans and the oats. Figure on about 1 tablespoon (three 1-teaspoon additions) for the smaller batch, with proportional increases for the other batches. A little too much olive oil can't hurt, but a dry paste will fall apart as it cooks and a far-too-wet paste will stick to the basket.
3. Scrape down and remove the blade. Using clean, wet hands, form the paste into two 10 cm patties for the small batch, three 10 cm patties for the medium, or four 10 cm patties for the large batch, setting them one by one on a cutting board. Generously coat both sides of the patties with olive oil spray.
4. Set them in the basket in one layer. Air-fry undisturbed for 10 minutes, or until lightly browned and crisp at the edges.
5. Use a nonstick-safe spatula, and perhaps a flat-ware fork for balance, to transfer the burgers to a wire rack. Cool for 5 minutes before serving.

Variations & Ingredients Tips:

- Add finely chopped vegetables like bell peppers, onions, or carrots for extra flavor and nutrition.
- Experiment with different spices and herbs, such as smoked paprika, garlic powder, or cilantro.
- For a gluten-free version, ensure all ingredients are certified gluten-free.

Per Serving: Calories: 280; Cholesterol: 0mg; Total Fat: 15g; Saturated Fat: 2g; Sodium: 420mg; Total Carbohydrates: 28g; Dietary Fiber: 8g; Total Sugars: 2g; Protein: 10g

Appetizers And Snacks

Chicken Shawarma Bites

Servings: 6 | Prep Time: 10 Minutes | Cooking Time: 22 Minutes

Ingredients:

- 680 g Boneless skinless chicken thighs, trimmed of any fat and cut into 2.5 cm pieces
- 1½ tablespoons Olive oil
- Up to 1½ tablespoons Minced garlic
- ½ teaspoon Table salt
- ¼ teaspoon Ground cardamom
- ¼ teaspoon Ground cinnamon
- ¼ teaspoon Ground cumin
- ¼ teaspoon Mild paprika
- Up to a ¼ teaspoon Grated nutmeg
- ¼ teaspoon Ground black pepper

Directions:

1. Preheat the air fryer to 200°C/400°F.
2. Mix all the ingredients in a large bowl until the chicken is thoroughly and evenly coated in the oil and spices.
3. When the machine is at temperature, scrape the coated chicken pieces into the basket and spread them out into one layer as much as you can. Air-fry for 22 minutes, shaking the basket at least three times during cooking to rearrange the pieces, until well browned and crisp.
4. Pour the chicken pieces onto a wire rack. Cool for 5 minutes before serving.

Variations & Ingredients Tips:

- Serve in pita bread with lettuce, tomatoes and garlic sauce.
- Use boneless skinless chicken breasts for a leaner option.
- Add a squeeze of lemon juice before serving for brightness.

Per Serving: Calories: 238; Total Fat: 13g; Saturated Fat: 3g; Cholesterol: 129mg; Sodium: 301mg; Total Carbs: 1g; Dietary Fiber: 0g; Total Sugars: 0g; Protein: 29g

Nicoise Deviled Eggs

Servings: 4 | Prep Time: 10 Minutes | Cooking Time: 20 Minutes

Ingredients:

- 4 eggs
- 2 tbsp mayonnaise
- 10 chopped Nicoise olives
- 2 tbsp goat cheese
- crumbles
- Salt and pepper to taste
- 2 tbsp chopped parsley

Directions:

1. Preheat air fryer to 130°C/260°F. Place the eggs in silicone muffin cups to avoid bumping around and cracking during the cooking process. Add silicone cups to the frying basket and air fry for 15 minutes. Remove and run the eggs under cold water. When cool, remove the shells and halve them lengthwise. Spoon yolks into a separate medium bowl and arrange white halves on a large plate. Mash the yolks with a fork. Stir in the remaining ingredients. Spoon mixture into white halves and scatter with mint to serve.

Variations & Ingredients Tips:

- Substitute Kalamata olives for Nicoise olives for a different briny flavor.
- Try using feta cheese instead of goat cheese for a saltier taste.
- Add a dash of hot sauce or Dijon mustard to the yolk mixture for extra zing.

Per Serving: Calories: 124; Total Fat: 10g; Saturated Fat: 3g; Cholesterol: 191mg; Sodium: 236mg; Total Carbs: 1g; Dietary Fiber: 0g; Total Sugars: 0g; Protein: 7g

Sausage And Cheese Rolls

Servings: 3 | Prep Time: 15 Minutes | Cooking Time: 18 Minutes

Ingredients:

- 3 (85-99g) sweet or hot Italian sausage links
- 2 (28g) string cheese sticks, unwrapped and cut in half lengthwise
- 3/4 (412g) thawed sheet frozen puff pastry, from one 490g box

Directions:

1. Preheat the air fryer to 200°C/400°F. When at temperature, set the sausage links in the basket and air-fry undisturbed for 12 minutes, or until cooked through. Use tongs to transfer links to a wire rack. Cool for 15 minutes. Cut links in half lengthwise. Sandwich half a string cheese stick between two sausage halves, trimming ends so cheese doesn't stick out. Roll each puff pastry piece into a 15x15cm square on work surface. Set sausage-cheese sandwich at one edge and roll up in dough, ends open. Repeat with remaining pastry, sausage, and cheese. Set rolls seam-side down in basket. Air-fry at 200°C/400°F for 6 minutes, until puffed and golden. Use nonstick spatula to transfer rolls to wire rack. Cool 5 minutes before serving.

Variations & Ingredients Tips:

- Try different sausage flavors like maple or andouille.
- Brush with egg wash before air frying for a glossy finish.
- Serve with mustard or marinara sauce for dipping.

Per Serving: Calories: 548; Total Fat: 37g; Saturated Fat: 14g; Cholesterol: 69mg; Sodium: 1153mg; Total Carbs: 31g; Dietary Fiber: 1g; Total Sugars: 3g; Protein: 21g

Roasted Red Pepper Dip

Servings: 2 | Prep Time: 10 Minutes | Cooking Time: 15 Minutes

Ingredients:

- 2 medium-size red bell peppers
- 425 g canned white beans, drained and rinsed
- 1 tbsp fresh oregano
- leaves, packed
- 3 tbsp olive oil
- 1 tbsp lemon juice
- ½ tsp table salt
- ½ tsp ground black pepper

Directions:

1. Preheat the air fryer to 200°C/400°F. Set the peppers in the basket and air-fry undisturbed for 15 minutes, until blistered and even blackened. Use kitchen tongs to transfer the peppers to a zip-closed plastic bag or small bowl. Seal the bag or cover the bowl with plastic wrap. Set aside for 20 minutes. Peel each pepper, then stem it, cut it in half, and remove all its seeds and their white membranes. Set the pieces of the pepper in a food processor. Add the beans, oregano, olive oil, lemon juice, salt, and pepper. Cover and process until smooth, stopping the machine at least once to scrape down the inside of the canister. Scrape the dip into a bowl and serve warm, or cover and refrigerate for up to 3 days (although the dip tastes best if it's allowed to come back to room temperature).

Variations & Ingredients Tips:

- Roast a head of garlic along with the peppers and add the cloves to the dip for a deeper flavor.

- Use cannellini beans, chickpeas, or black beans instead of white beans for a different taste and texture.
- Add smoked paprika, cumin, or hot sauce for a smoky or spicy kick.

Per Serving: Calories: 437; Total Fat: 22g; Saturated Fat: 3g; Cholesterol: 0mg; Sodium: 886mg; Total Carbs: 47g; Dietary Fiber: 12g; Total Sugars: 3g; Protein: 17g

Wrapped Smokies In Bacon

Servings: 4 | Prep Time: 5 Minutes | Cooking Time: 15 Minutes

Ingredients:

- 8 small smokies
- 8 bacon strips, sliced
- Salt and pepper to taste

Directions:

1. Preheat air fryer to 175°C/350°F. Wrap the bacon slices around smokies. Arrange the rolls, seam side down, on the greased frying basket. Sprinkle with salt and pepper and air fry for 5-8 minutes, turning once until the bacon is crisp and juicy around them. Serve and enjoy!

Variations & Ingredients Tips:

- Use turkey bacon, prosciutto, or pancetta instead of regular bacon for a twist.
- Brush the wrapped smokies with maple syrup, honey, or brown sugar before cooking for a sweet and savory combo.
- Serve with mustard, ketchup, or BBQ sauce for dipping.

Per Serving: Calories: 186; Total Fat: 15g; Saturated Fat: 5g; Cholesterol: 32mg; Sodium: 578mg; Total Carbohydrates: 1g; Dietary Fiber: 0g; Total Sugars: 0g; Protein: 9g

Red Potato Chips With Mexican Dip

Servings: 6 | Prep Time: 15 Minutes | Cooking Time: 35 Minutes

Ingredients:

- 1 tsp smoked paprika
- 1 tbsp lemon juice
- 10 purple red potatoes
- 1 tsp olive oil
- 2 tsp minced thyme
- ⅛ tsp cayenne pepper
- Sea salt to taste
- 1 cup Greek yogurt
- 2 chipotle chiles, minced
- 2 tbsp adobo sauce

Directions:

1. Preheat air fryer to 200°C/400°F. Cut the potatoes lengthwise in thin strips and put them in a bowl. Spray olive oil all over them and toss until the strips are evenly coated. Add the potatoes to the frying basket and air fry for 9-14 minutes. Use a metal spoon to mix them up at around minute 5. Mix the yogurt, chipotle chiles, adobo sauce, paprika, and lemon juice in a bowl, then put it in the refrigerator. When cooking is finished, put the potatoes on a large plate and toss thyme, cayenne pepper, and sea salt on top. Serve with this Mexican dip. Enjoy!

Variations & Ingredients Tips:

- Add grated garlic, lime juice, or chopped cilantro to the dip for extra flavor.
- Experiment with different types of potatoes like Yukon Gold, fingerling, or sweet potatoes.
- For a vegan version, use dairy-free yogurt or cashew cream instead of Greek yogurt.

Per Serving: Calories: 154; Total Fat: 3g; Saturated Fat: 1g; Cholesterol: 0mg; Sodium: 314mg; Total Carbs: 27g; Dietary Fiber: 3g; Total Sugars: 3g; Protein: 6g

Olive & Pepper Tapenade

Servings: 4 | Prep Time: 10 Minutes | Cooking Time: 10 Minutes

Ingredients:

- 1 red bell pepper
- 3 tbsp olive oil
- ½ cup black olives, chopped
- 1 garlic clove, minced
- ½ tsp dried oregano
- 1 tbsp white wine juice

Directions:

1. Preheat air fryer to 190°C/380°F. Lightly brush the outside of the bell pepper with some olive oil and put it in the frying basket. Roast for 5 minutes. Combine the remaining olive oil with olives, garlic, oregano, and white wine in a bowl. Remove the red pepper from the air fryer, then gently slice off the stem and discard the seeds. Chop into small pieces. Add the chopped pepper to the olive mixture and stir all together until combined. Serve and enjoy!

Variations & Ingredients Tips:

- Use green olives or a mixture of olives for a different flavor profile.
- Add anchovies or capers for a salty, briny kick.
- Serve with crostini, pita chips, or fresh vegetables for dipping.

Per Serving: Calories: 137; Total Fat: 14g; Saturated Fat: 2g; Cholesterol: no data; Sodium: 204mg; Total Carbs: 4g; Dietary Fiber: 1g; Total Sugars: 1g; Protein: 1g

Garlic Parmesan Kale Chips

Servings: 2 | Prep Time: 5 Minutes | Cooking Time: 6 Minutes

Ingredients:

- 16 large kale leaves, washed and thick stems removed
- 1 tablespoon avocado oil
- ½ teaspoon garlic powder
- 1 teaspoon soy sauce or tamari
- ¼ cup grated Parmesan cheese

Directions:

1. Preheat the air fryer to 190°C/370°F.

2. Make a stack of kale leaves and cut them into 4 pieces.

3. Place the kale pieces into a large bowl. Drizzle the avocado oil onto the kale and rub to coat. Add the garlic powder, soy sauce or tamari, and cheese, tossing to coat.

4. Pour the chips into the air fryer basket and cook for 3 minutes, shake the basket, and cook another 3 minutes, checking for crispness every minute. When done cooking, pour the kale chips onto paper towels and cool at least 5 minutes before serving.

Variations & Ingredients Tips:

- Use spinach, Swiss chard or collard greens instead of kale.
- Add some smoked paprika, nutritional yeast or lemon zest for extra flavor.
- Store leftovers in an airtight container at room temperature for up to 3 days.

Per Serving: Calories: 160; Total Fat: 13g; Saturated Fat: 3g; Cholesterol: 11mg; Sodium: 520mg; Total Carbs: 7g; Dietary Fiber: 2g; Total Sugars: 1g; Protein: 6g

Homemade French Fries

Servings: 2 | Prep Time: 15 Minutes | Cooking Time: 25 Minutes

Ingredients:

- 2 to 3 russet potatoes, peeled and cut into 13 mm sticks
- 2 to 3 teaspoons olive or vegetable oil
- salt

Directions:

1. Bring a large saucepan of salted water to a boil on the stovetop while you peel and cut the potatoes. Blanch the potatoes in the boiling salted water for 4 minutes while you Preheat the air fryer to 200°C/400°F. Strain the potatoes and rinse them with cold water. Dry them well with a clean kitchen towel.

2. Toss the dried potato sticks gently with the oil and place them in the air fryer basket. Air-fry

for 25 minutes, shaking the basket a few times while the fries cook to help them brown evenly. Season the fries with salt mid-way through cooking and serve them warm with tomato ketchup, Sriracha mayonnaise or a mix of lemon zest, Parmesan cheese and parsley.

Variations & Ingredients Tips:

● Use sweet potatoes, parsnips or turnips instead of russets.
● Season the fries with garlic powder, onion powder or Old Bay seasoning.
● Serve with malt vinegar, truffle aioli or chimichurri sauce for dipping.

Per Serving: Calories: 266; Total Fat: 7g; Saturated Fat: 1g; Cholesterol: 0mg; Sodium: 12mg; Total Carbs: 48g; Dietary Fiber: 5g; Total Sugars: 2g; Protein: 5g

Paprika Onion Blossom

Servings: 4 | Prep Time: 20 Minutes | Cooking Time: 35 Minutes + Cooling Time

Ingredients:

● 1 large onion
● 1½ cups flour
● 1 tsp garlic powder
● 1 tsp paprika
● ½ tsp bell pepper
  powder
● Salt and pepper to taste
● 2 eggs
● 1 cup milk

Directions:

1. Remove the tip of the onion but leave the root base intact. Peel the onion to the root and remove skin. Place the onion cut-side down on a cutting board. Starting 3 cm down from the root, cut down to the bottom. Repeat until the onion is divided into quarters. Starting 1.3 cm down from the root, repeat the cuts in between the first cuts. Repeat this process in between the cuts until you have 16 cuts in the onion. Flip the onion onto the root and carefully spread the inner layers. Set aside. In a bowl, add flour, garlic, paprika, bell pepper, salt, and pepper, then stir. In another large bowl, whisk eggs and milk.

Place the onion in the flour bowl and cover with flour mixture. Transfer the onion into the egg mixture and coat completely with either a spoon or basting brush. Return the onion to the flour bowl and cover completely. Take a sheet of foil and wrap the onion with the foil. Freeze for 45 minutes. Preheat air fryer to 200°C/400°F. Remove the onion from the foil and place in the greased frying basket. Air fry for 10 minutes. Lightly spray the onion with cooking oil, then cook for another 10-15 minutes. Serve immediately.

Variations & Ingredients Tips:

● Experiment with different spice blends like Cajun, Italian, or Mexican for varied flavors.
● For a cheesy version, sprinkle grated Parmesan or cheddar cheese over the onion during the last few minutes of cooking.
● Serve with a dipping sauce like ranch, blue cheese, or chipotle mayo.

Per Serving: Calories: 301; Total Fat: 6g; Saturated Fat: 2g; Cholesterol: 97mg; Sodium: 91mg; Total Carbs: 51g; Dietary Fiber: 3g; Total Sugars: 6g; Protein: 11g

Tasty Roasted Black Olives & Tomatoes

Servings: 6 | Prep Time: 10 Minutes | Cooking Time: 25 Minutes

Ingredients:

● 2 cups grape tomatoes
● 4 garlic cloves, chopped
● ½ red onion, chopped
● 1 cup black olives
● 1 cup green olives
● 1 tbsp thyme, minced
● 1 tbsp oregano, minced
● 2 tbsp olive oil
● ½ tsp salt

Directions:

1. Preheat air fryer to 190°C/380°F. Add all ingredients to a bowl and toss well to coat. Pour the mixture into the frying basket and roast for 10

minutes. Stir the mixture, then roast for an additional 10 minutes. Serve and enjoy!

Variations & Ingredients Tips:

- Add crumbled feta cheese, pine nuts, or capers for a Mediterranean flair.
- Serve over pasta, rice, or crusty bread for a heartier dish.
- Use different types of olives like Kalamata, Castelvetrano, or Niçoise for varied flavors.

Per Serving: Calories: 118; Total Fat: 10g; Saturated Fat: 1g; Sodium: 525mg; Total Carbohydrates: 6g; Dietary Fiber: 2g; Total Sugars: 2g; Protein: 1g

Avocado Egg Rolls

Servings: 8 | Prep Time: 25 Minutes | Cooking Time: 8 Minutes

Ingredients:

- 8 full-size egg roll wrappers
- 1 medium avocado, sliced into 8 pieces
- 1 cup cooked black beans, divided
- ½ cup mild salsa, divided
- ½ cup shredded Mexican cheese, divided
- 80 ml filtered water, divided
- ½ cup sour cream
- 1 teaspoon chipotle hot sauce

Directions:

1. Preheat the air fryer to 200°C/400°F.
2. Place the egg roll wrapper on a flat surface and place 1 strip of avocado down in the center.
3. Top the avocado with 2 tablespoons of black beans, 1 tablespoon of salsa, and 1 tablespoon of shredded cheese.
4. Place two of your fingers into the water, and then moisten the four outside edges of the egg roll wrapper with water (so the outer edges will secure shut).
5. Fold the bottom corner up, covering the filling. Then secure the sides over the top, remembering to lightly moisten them so they stick. Tightly roll the egg roll up and moisten the final flap of the wrapper and firmly press it into the egg

roll to secure it shut.
6. Repeat Steps 2–5 until all 8 egg rolls are complete.
7. When ready to cook, spray the air fryer basket with olive oil spray and place the egg rolls into the basket. Depending on the size and type of air fryer you have, you may need to do this in two sets.
8. Cook for 4 minutes, flip, and then cook the remaining 4 minutes.
9. Repeat until all the egg rolls are cooked. Meanwhile, mix the sour cream with the hot sauce to serve as a dipping sauce.
10. Serve warm.

Variations & Ingredients Tips:

- Add some cooked shredded chicken or pork to the filling.
- Use pepper jack cheese for extra spice.
- Serve with guacamole or queso dip.

Per Serving: Calories: 226; Total Fat: 11g; Saturated Fat: 4g; Cholesterol: 17mg; Sodium: 473mg; Total Carbs: 25g; Dietary Fiber: 4g; Total Sugars: 2g; Protein: 7g

Artichoke Samosas

Servings: 6 | Prep Time: 20 Minutes | Cooking Time: 25 Minutes

Ingredients:

- ½ cup minced artichoke hearts
- ¼ cup ricotta cheese
- 1 egg white
- 3 tbsp grated mozzarella
- ½ tsp dried thyme
- 6 phyllo dough sheets
- 2 tbsp melted butter
- 1 cup mango chutney

Directions:

1. Preheat air fryer to 200°C/400°F. Mix together ricotta cheese, egg white, artichoke hearts, mozzarella cheese, and thyme in a small bowl until well blended. When you bring out the phyllo dough, cover it with a damp kitchen towel so that it doesn't dry out while you are working with it. Take one sheet of phyllo and place it on

the work surface.

2. Cut it into thirds lengthwise. At the base of each strip, place about 7 g of filling. Fold the bottom right-hand tip of the strip over to the left-hand side to make a triangle. Continue flipping and folding triangles along the strip. Brush the triangle with butter to seal the edges. Place triangles in the greased frying basket and Bake until golden and crisp, 4 minutes. Serve with mango chutney.

Variations & Ingredients Tips:

- Try using spinach, mushrooms or potatoes for the filling.
- Serve with a mint-yogurt dip or tamarind chutney.
- For a vegan version, substitute tofu for the cheeses.

Per Serving: Calories: 202; Cholesterol: 18mg; Total Fat: 10g; Saturated Fat: 6g; Sodium: 231mg; Total Carbohydrates: 23g; Dietary Fiber: 1g; Total Sugars: 11g; Protein: 5g

Cuban Sliders

Servings: 8 | Prep Time: 10 Minutes | Cooking Time: 8 Minutes

Ingredients:

- 8 slices ciabatta bread, 6 mm thick
- cooking spray
- 1 tablespoon brown mustard
- 170-225 g thin sliced leftover roast
- pork
- 115 g thin deli turkey
- ⅓ cup bread and butter pickle slices
- 60-85 g Pepper Jack cheese slices

Directions:

1. Spray one side of each slice of bread with butter or olive oil cooking spray.
2. Spread brown mustard on other side of each slice.
3. Layer pork roast, turkey, pickles, and cheese on 4 of the slices. Top with remaining slices.
4. Cook at 200°C/390°F for approximately 8 min-

utes. The sandwiches should be golden brown.

5. Cut each slider in half to make 8 portions.

Variations & Ingredients Tips:

- Use ham, prosciutto or salami instead of turkey.
- Add some sliced pickled jalapeños or banana peppers for spice.
- Brush the tops with garlic butter or sprinkle with everything bagel seasoning before cooking.

Per Serving: Calories: 218; Total Fat: 9g; Saturated Fat: 4g; Cholesterol: 33mg; Sodium: 556mg; Total Carbs: 21g; Dietary Fiber: 1g; Total Sugars: 2g; Protein: 13g

Potato Chips

Servings: 2 | Prep Time: 10 Minutes | Cooking Time: 15 Minutes

Ingredients:

- 2 medium potatoes
- 2 tsp extra-light olive oil
- oil for misting or cooking spray
- salt and pepper

Directions:

1. Peel the potatoes. Using a mandoline or paring knife, shave potatoes into thin slices, dropping them into a bowl of water as you cut them. Dry potatoes as thoroughly as possible with paper towels or a clean dish towel. Toss potato slices with the oil to coat completely. Spray air fryer basket with cooking spray and add potato slices. Stir and separate with a fork. Cook at 200°C/390°F for 5 minutes. Stir and separate potato slices. Cook 5 more minutes. Stir and separate potatoes again. Cook another 5 minutes. Season to taste.

Variations & Ingredients Tips:

- Use sweet potatoes or root vegetables like beets or parsnips for a colorful twist.
- Season the chips with different spice blends like ranch, BBQ, or sour cream and onion.
- For a healthier option, use less oil or try making chips with just cooking spray.

Per Serving: Calories: 154; Total Fat: 7g; Saturated Fat: 1g; Cholesterol: no data; Sodium: 6mg; Total Carbs: 22g; Dietary Fiber: 2g; Total Sugars: 1g; Protein: 2g

Fried Pickles

Servings: 2 | Prep Time: 10 Minutes | Cooking Time: 15 Minutes

Ingredients:

- 1 egg
- 1 tablespoon milk
- ¼ teaspoon hot sauce
- 2 cups sliced
- dill pickles, well drained
- ¾ cup breadcrumbs
- oil for misting or cooking spray

Directions:

1. Preheat air fryer to 200°C/390°F.
2. Beat together egg, milk, and hot sauce in a bowl large enough to hold all the pickles.
3. Add pickles to the egg wash and stir well to coat.
4. Place breadcrumbs in a large plastic bag or container with lid.
5. Drain egg wash from pickles and place them in bag with breadcrumbs. Shake to coat.
6. Pile pickles into air fryer basket and spray with oil.
7. Cook for 5 minutes. Shake basket and spray with oil.
8. Cook 5 more minutes. Shake and spray again. Separate any pickles that have stuck together and mist any spots you've missed.
9. Cook for 5 minutes longer or until dark golden brown and crispy.

Variations & Ingredients Tips:

- Use panko breadcrumbs for a crunchier texture.
- Add some garlic powder, onion powder or cayenne pepper to the breading.
- Serve with ranch dressing, blue cheese dip or chipotle mayo for dipping.

Per Serving: Calories: 265; Total Fat: 12g; Saturated Fat: 3g; Cholesterol: 93mg; Sodium:

1769mg; Total Carbs: 29g; Dietary Fiber: 2g; Total Sugars: 5g; Protein: 9g

Buffalo Cauliflower

Servings: 6 | Prep Time: 10 Minutes | Cooking Time: 12 Minutes

Ingredients:

- 1 large head of cauliflower, washed and cut into medium-size florets
- ½ cup all-purpose flour
- ¼ cup melted butter
- 3 tablespoons hot sauce
- ½ teaspoon garlic powder
- ½ cup blue cheese dip or ranch dressing (optional)

Directions:

1. Preheat the air fryer to 175°C/350°F.
2. Make sure the cauliflower florets are dry, and then coat them in flour.
3. Liberally spray the air fryer basket with an olive oil mist. Place the cauliflower into the basket, making sure not to stack them on top of each other. Depending on the size of your air fryer, you may need to do this in two batches.
4. Cook for 6 minutes, then shake the basket, and cook another 6 minutes.
5. While cooking, mix the melted butter, hot sauce, and garlic powder in a large bowl.
6. Carefully remove the cauliflower from the air fryer. Toss the cauliflower into the butter mixture to coat. Repeat Steps 2–4 for any leftover cauliflower. Serve warm with the dip of your choice.

Variations & Ingredients Tips:

- Use broccoli florets instead of cauliflower for a different vegetable option.
- Adjust the amount of hot sauce to make it milder or spicier.
- Sprinkle with crumbled blue cheese or Parmesan before serving.

Per Serving: Calories: 137; Total Fat: 9g; Saturated Fat: 5g; Cholesterol: 20mg; Sodium: 416mg;

Total Carbs: 12g; Dietary Fiber: 3g; Total Sugars: 3g; Protein: 4g

Honey Tater Tots With Bacon

Servings: 4 | Prep Time: 5 Minutes | Cooking Time: 25 Minutes

Ingredients:

- 24 frozen tater tots
- 6 bacon slices
- 1 tbsp honey
- 1 cup grated cheddar

Directions:

1. Preheat air fryer to 200°C/400°F. Air Fry the tater tots for 10 minutes, shaking the basket once halfway through cooking. Cut the bacon into pieces. When the tater tots are done, remove them from the fryer to a baking pan. Top them with bacon and drizzle with honey. Air Fry for 5 minutes to crisp up the bacon. Top the tater tots with cheese and cook for 2 minutes to melt the cheese. Serve.

Variations & Ingredients Tips:

- Use sweet potato tater tots for a healthier twist.
- Add some chopped green onions or jalapeños for extra flavor.
- Drizzle with ranch dressing or BBQ sauce before serving.

Per Serving: Calories: 342; Total Fat: 21g; Saturated Fat: 9g; Cholesterol: 47mg; Sodium: 691mg; Total Carbs: 26g; Dietary Fiber: 1g; Total Sugars: 6g; Protein: 14g

Savory Eggplant Fries

Servings: 4 | Prep Time: 10 Minutes | Cooking Time: 20 Minutes

Ingredients:

- 1 eggplant, sliced
- 2 1/2 tbsp soy sauce
- 2 tsp garlic powder
- 2 tsp onion powder
- 4 tsp olive oil
- 2 tbsp fresh basil, chopped

Directions:

1. Preheat air fryer to 200°C/390°F. Place the eggplant slices in a bowl and sprinkle the soy sauce, garlic, onion, and oil on top. Coat the eggplant evenly. Place the eggplant in a single layer in the greased frying basket and Air Fry for 5 minutes. Remove and put the eggplant in the bowl again. Toss the eggplant slices to coat evenly with the remaining liquid and put back in the fryer. Roast for another 3 minutes. Remove the basket and flip the pieces over to ensure even cooking. Roast for another 5 minutes or until the eggplant is golden. Top with basil and serve.

Variations & Ingredients Tips:

- Use breadcrumbs or panko for extra crunch.
- Add grated parmesan on top after cooking.
- Serve with marinara sauce for dipping.

Per Serving: Calories: 101; Total Fat: 7g; Saturated Fat: 1g; Cholesterol: 0mg; Sodium: 670mg; Total Carbs: 9g; Dietary Fiber: 3g; Total Sugars: 4g; Protein: 2g

Piri Piri Chicken Wings

Servings: 4 | Prep Time: 10 Minutes | Cooking Time: 45 Minutes

Ingredients:

- 1 cup crushed cracker crumbs
- 1 tbsp sweet paprika
- 1 tbsp smoked paprika
- 1 tbsp Piri Piri seasoning
- 1 tsp sea salt
- 2 tsp onion powder
- 1 tsp garlic powder
- 910 g chicken drumettes
- 2 tbsp olive oil

Directions:

1. Preheat the air fryer to 190°C/380°F. Combine the cracker crumbs, paprikas, Piri Piri seasoning, sea salt, onion and garlic powders in a bowl and mix well. Pour into a screw-top glass jar and set aside. Put the drumettes in a large bowl, drizzle with the olive oil, and toss to coat. Sprinkle ⅓ cup of the breading mix over the

meat and press the mix into the drumettes. Put half the drumettes in the frying basket and air fry for 20-25 minutes, shaking the basket once until golden and crisp. Serve hot.

Variations & Ingredients Tips:

● Adjust the amount of Piri Piri seasoning to make the wings milder or spicier.

● Use chicken wings instead of drumettes for a different presentation.

● Serve with ranch or blue cheese dressing for dipping.

Per Serving: Calories: 514; Total Fat: 36g; Saturated Fat: 8g; Cholesterol: 158mg; Sodium: 1020mg; Total Carbs: 13g; Dietary Fiber: 2g; Total Sugars: 1g; Protein: 36g

Vegetarian Recipes

Party Giant Nachos

Servings: 2 | Prep Time: 10 Minutes | Cooking Time: 20 Minutes

Ingredients:

- 2 tbsp sour cream
- ½ tsp chili powder
- Salt to taste
- 2 soft corn tortillas
- 2 tsp avocado oil
- ½ cup refried beans
- ¼ cup cheddar cheese shreds
- 2 tbsp Parmesan
- cheese
- 2 tbsp sliced black olives
- ¼ cup torn iceberg lettuce
- ¼ cup baby spinach
- ½ sliced avocado
- 1 tomato, diced
- 2 lime wedges

Directions:

1. Preheat air fryer at 200°C/400°F.
2. Whisk the sour cream, chili powder, and salt in a small bowl.
3. Brush tortillas with avocado oil and season one side with salt. Place tortillas in the air fryer basket and Bake for 3 minutes. Set aside.
4. Layer the refried beans, Parmesan and cheddar cheeses in the tortillas. Place them back into the basket and Bake for 2 minutes.
5. Divide tortillas into 2 serving plates. Top each tortilla with black olives, baby spinach, lettuce, and tomatoes. Dollop sour cream mixture on each.
6. Serve with lime and avocado wedges on the side.

Variations & Ingredients Tips:

● Add sliced jalapeños or hot sauce for a spicy kick.

● Use Greek yogurt instead of sour cream for a healthier option.

● Substitute refried beans with black beans or pinto beans.

Per Serving: Calories: 380; Total Fat: 24g; Saturated Fat: 7g; Sodium: 780mg; Total Carbohydrates: 32g; Dietary Fiber: 9g; Total Sugars: 5g; Protein: 13g

Charred Cauliflower Tacos

Servings: 4 | Prep Time: 15 Minutes | Cooking Time: 10 Minutes

Ingredients:

- 1 head cauliflower, washed and cut into florets
- 2 tablespoons avocado oil
- 2 teaspoons taco
- seasoning
- 1 medium avocado
- ½ teaspoon garlic powder
- ¼ teaspoon black pepper

- ¼ teaspoon salt
- 2 tablespoons chopped red onion
- 2 teaspoons fresh squeezed lime juice
- ¼ cup chopped cilantro
- Eight 15-cm corn tortillas
- ½ cup cooked corn
- ½ cup shredded purple cabbage

Directions:

1. Preheat the air fryer to 200°C/390°F.
2. In a large bowl, toss the cauliflower with the avocado oil and taco seasoning. Set the metal trivet inside the air fryer basket and liberally spray with olive oil.
3. Place the cauliflower onto the trivet and cook for 10 minutes, shaking every 3 minutes to allow for an even char.
4. While the cauliflower is cooking, prepare the avocado sauce. In a medium bowl, mash the avocado; then mix in the garlic powder, pepper, salt, and onion. Stir in the lime juice and cilantro; set aside.
5. Remove the cauliflower from the air fryer basket.
6. Place 1 tablespoon of avocado sauce in the middle of a tortilla, and top with corn, cabbage, and charred cauliflower. Repeat with the remaining tortillas. Serve immediately.

Variations & Ingredients Tips:

- Use broccoli, Brussels sprouts, or carrots instead of cauliflower for different veggie options.
- Add sliced radish, pickled onions, or queso fresco for extra toppings.
- Serve with salsa, hot sauce, or lime wedges on the side.

Per Serving (2 tacos): Calories: 380; Cholesterol: 0mg; Total Fat: 20g; Saturated Fat: 3g; Sodium: 520mg; Total Carbohydrates: 47g; Dietary Fiber: 11g; Total Sugars: 7g; Protein: 8g

Colorful Vegetable Medley

Servings: 4 | Prep Time: 10 Minutes | Cooking Time: 20 Minutes

Ingredients:

- 455g green beans, chopped
- 2 carrots, cubed
- Salt and pepper to taste
- 1 zucchini, cut into chunks
- 1 red bell pepper, sliced

Directions:

1. Preheat air fryer to 200°C/390°F. Combine green beans, carrots, salt and pepper in a large bowl. Spray with cooking oil and transfer to the frying basket. Roast for 6 minutes.
2. Combine zucchini and red pepper in a bowl. Season to taste and spray with cooking oil; set aside. When the cooking time is up, add the zucchini and red pepper to the basket. Cook for another 6 minutes.
3. Serve and enjoy.

Variations & Ingredients Tips:

- Add diced potatoes or sweet potatoes for extra heartiness.
- Substitute green beans with asparagus or broccolini.
- Toss with balsamic vinegar or lemon juice before serving for extra flavor.

Per Serving: Calories: 80; Total Fat: 0.5g; Saturated Fat: 0g; Cholesterol: 0mg; Sodium: 70mg; Total Carbs: 16g; Dietary Fiber: 6g; Total Sugars: 8g; Protein: 4g

Tacos

Servings: 24 | Prep Time: 20 Minutes | Cooking Time: 8 Minutes Per Batch

Ingredients:

- 1 24-count package 10-cm corn tortillas
- 1½ cups refried beans (about ¾ of a 425-gram can)
- 113 grams sharp
- Cheddar cheese, grated
- ½ cup salsa
- oil for misting or cooking spray

Directions:

1. Preheat air fryer to 200°C/390°F.
2. Wrap refrigerated tortillas in damp paper towels and microwave for 30 to 60 seconds to warm. If necessary, rewarm tortillas as you go to keep them soft enough to fold without breaking.
3. Working with one tortilla at a time, top with 1 tablespoon of beans, 1 tablespoon of grated cheese, and 1 teaspoon of salsa. Fold over and press down very gently on the center. Press edges firmly all around to seal. Spray both sides with oil or cooking spray.
4. Cooking in two batches, place half the tacos in the air fryer basket. To cook 12 at a time, you may need to stand them upright and lean some against the sides of basket. It's okay if they're crowded as long as you leave a little room for air to circulate around them.
5. Cook for 8 minutes or until golden brown and crispy.
6. Repeat steps 4 and 5 to cook remaining tacos.

Variations & Ingredients Tips:

- Use black beans, pinto beans, or vegetarian chili instead of refried beans.
- Add diced avocado, shredded lettuce, or chopped tomatoes as additional fillings.
- Serve with guacamole, sour cream, or hot sauce on the side.

Per Serving: Calories: 80; Total Fat: 3g; Saturated Fat: 1.5g; Sodium: 180mg; Total Carbohydrates: 10g; Dietary Fiber: 2g; Total Sugars: 1g; Protein: 3g

Lentil Burritos With Cilantro Chutney

Servings: 4 | Prep Time: 20 Minutes | Cooking Time: 30 Minutes

Ingredients:

- 1 cup cilantro chutney
- 454 grams cooked potatoes, mashed
- 2 tsp sunflower oil
- 3 garlic cloves, minced
- 1 ½ tbsp fresh lime juice
- 1 ½ tsp cumin powder
- 1 tsp onion powder
- 1 tsp coriander powder
- Salt to taste
- ½ tsp turmeric
- ¼ tsp cayenne powder
- 4 large flour tortillas
- 1 cup cooked lentils
- ½ cup shredded cabbage
- ¼ cup minced red onions

Directions:

1. Preheat air fryer to 200°C/390°F.
2. Place the mashed potatoes, sunflower oil, garlic, lime, cumin, onion powder, coriander, salt, turmeric, and cayenne in a large bowl. Stir well until combined.
3. Lay the tortillas out flat on the counter. In the middle of each, distribute the potato filling. Add some of the lentils, cabbage, and red onions on top of the potatoes.
4. Close the wraps by folding the bottom of the tortillas up and over the filling, then folding the sides in, then roll the bottom up to form a burrito.
5. Place the wraps in the greased air fryer basket, seam side down. Air Fry for 6-8 minutes, flipping once until golden and crispy.
6. Serve topped with cilantro chutney.

Variations & Ingredients Tips:

- Make your own cilantro chutney by blending fresh cilantro, mint, green chili, lime juice, and salt.
- Use kidney beans or black beans instead of lentils for variation.
- Add shredded cheese to the filling for extra richness and flavor.

Per Serving: Calories: 510; Total Fat: 13g; Saturated Fat: 2g; Sodium: 820mg; Total Carbohydrates: 87g; Dietary Fiber: 13g; Total Sugars: 6g; Protein: 18g

Chicano Rice Bowls

Servings: 4 | Prep Time: 15 Minutes | Cooking Time: 10 Minutes

Ingredients:

- 1 cup sour cream
- 2 tbsp milk
- 1 tsp ground cumin
- 1 tsp chili powder
- 1/8 tsp cayenne pepper
- 1 tbsp tomato paste
- 1 white onion, chopped
- 1 clove garlic, minced
- ½ tsp ground tur-meric
- ½ tsp salt
- 1 cup canned black beans
- 1 cup canned corn kernels
- 1 tsp olive oil
- 4 cups cooked brown rice
- 3 tomatoes, diced
- 1 avocado, diced

Directions:

1. Whisk the sour cream, milk, cumin, ground turmeric, chili powder, cayenne pepper, and salt in a bowl. Let chill covered in the fridge until ready to use.
2. Preheat air fryer at 175°C/350°F. Combine beans, white onion, tomato paste, garlic, corn, and olive oil in a bowl. Transfer it into the frying basket and Air Fry for 5 minutes. Divide cooked rice into 4 serving bowls. Top each with bean mixture, tomatoes, and avocado and drizzle with sour cream mixture over. Serve immediately.

Variations & Ingredients Tips:

- Use quinoa, barley, or farro instead of brown rice for a different grain.
- Add shredded lettuce, salsa, or pickled jalapeños for extra toppings.
- Substitute sour cream with Greek yogurt or cashew cream for a lighter option.

Per Serving: Calories: 510; Cholesterol: 20mg; Total Fat: 22g; Saturated Fat: 8g; Sodium: 670mg; Total Carbohydrates: 70g; Dietary Fiber: 13g; Total Sugars: 9g; Protein: 15g

Veggie Fried Rice

Servings: 4 | Prep Time: 10 Minutes | Cooking Time: 25 Minutes

Ingredients:

- 1 cup cooked brown rice
- 1/3 cup chopped onion
- 1/2 cup chopped carrots
- 1/2 cup chopped bell peppers
- 1/2 cup chopped broccoli florets
- 3 tablespoons low-sodium soy sauce
- 1 tablespoon sesame oil
- 1 teaspoon ground ginger
- 1 teaspoon ground garlic powder
- 1/2 teaspoon black pepper
- 1/8 teaspoon salt
- 2 large eggs

Directions:

1. Preheat the air fryer to 190°C/370°F.
2. In a large bowl, mix together the brown rice, onions, carrots, bell pepper, and broccoli.
3. In a small bowl, whisk together the soy sauce, sesame oil, ginger, garlic powder, pepper, salt, and eggs.
4. Pour the egg mixture into the rice and vegetable mixture and mix together.
5. Liberally spray a 18-cm springform pan (or compatible air fryer dish) with olive oil. Add the rice mixture to the pan and cover with aluminum foil.
6. Place a metal trivet into the air fryer basket and set the pan on top. Cook for 15 minutes.
7. Carefully remove the pan from basket, discard the foil, and mix the rice. Return the rice to the air fryer basket, turning down the temperature to 180°C/350°F and cooking another 10 minutes.
8. Remove and let cool 5 minutes. Serve warm.

Variations & Ingredients Tips:

- Add diced tofu or edamame for extra protein.
- Use cauliflower rice for a low-carb option.
- Drizzle with sriracha or chili garlic sauce for heat.

Per Serving: Calories: 253; Total Fat: 8g; Saturated Fat: 1g; Sodium: 553mg; Total Carbohydrates: 38g; Dietary Fiber: 5g; Total Sugars: 5g; Protein: 8g

Creamy Broccoli & Mushroom Casserole

Servings: 4 | Prep Time: 10 Minutes | Cooking Time: 30 Minutes

Ingredients:

- 4 cups broccoli florets, chopped
- 1 cup crushed cheddar cheese crisps
- 1/4 cup diced onion
- 1/4 tsp dried thyme
- 1/4 tsp dried marjoram
- 1/4 tsp dried orega-no
- 1/2 cup diced mushrooms
- 1 egg
- 2 tbsp sour cream
- 1/4 cup mayonnaise
- Salt and pepper to taste

Directions:

1. Preheat air fryer to 175°C/350°F.
2. Combine all ingredients, except for the cheese crisps, in a bowl.
3. Spoon mixture into a round cake pan. Place cake pan in the frying basket and Bake for 14 minutes.
4. Let sit for 10 minutes. Distribute crushed cheddar cheese crisps over the top and serve.

Variations & Ingredients Tips:

- Add cooked bacon or ham for extra protein and flavor.
- Substitute sour cream with Greek yogurt for a tangy twist.
- Top with breadcrumbs or crushed crackers before baking for a crispy topping.

Per Serving: Calories: 210; Total Fat: 15g; Saturated Fat: 5g; Cholesterol: 55mg; Sodium: 330mg; Total Carbs: 13g; Dietary Fiber: 4g; Total Sugars: 3g; Protein: 8g

Hellenic Zucchini Bites

Servings:4 | Prep Time: 10 Minutes | Cooking Time: 20 Minutes

Ingredients:

- 8 pitted Kalamata olives, halved
- 2 tsp olive oil
- 1 zucchini, sliced
- ½ tsp salt
- ½ tsp Greek orega-no
- ½ cup marinara sauce
- ½ cup feta cheese crumbles
- 2 tbsp chopped dill

Directions:

1. Preheat air fryer to 180°C/350°F.
2. Brush olive oil over both sides of the zucchini circles. Lay out slices on a large plate and sprinkle with salt.
3. Then, top with marinara sauce, feta crumbles, Greek oregano and olives.
4. Place the topped circles in the air fryer basket and Air Fry for 5 minutes.
5. Garnish with chopped dill to serve.

Variations & Ingredients Tips:

- Use sliced eggplant or portobello mushroom caps instead of zucchini.
- Sprinkle with grated Parmesan or mozzarella cheese in addition to the feta.
- Drizzle with pesto sauce or olive tapenade for extra flavor.

Per Serving: Calories: 100; Total Fat: 8g; Saturated Fat: 3g; Sodium: 520mg; Total Carbohydrates: 5g; Dietary Fiber: 1g; Total Sugars: 3g; Protein: 3g

Vegan Buddha Bowls

Servings: 2 | Prep Time: 20 Minutes | Cooking Time: 45 Minutes

Ingredients:

- 1/2 cup quinoa
- 1 cup sweet potato cubes
- 340 grams broccoli florets
- 3/4 cup bread crumbs
- 1/4 cup chickpea flour
- 1/4 cup hot sauce
- 454 grams super-firm tofu, cubed
- 1 tsp lemon juice
- 2 tsp olive oil
- Salt to taste
- 2 scallions, thinly sliced
- 1 tbsp sesame seeds

Directions:

1. Preheat air fryer to 200°C/400°F.
2. Add quinoa and 1 cup of boiling water in a baking pan, cover it with aluminum foil, and Air Fry for 10 minutes. Set aside covered.
3. Put the sweet potatoes in the air fryer basket and Air Fry for 2 minutes. Add in broccoli and Air Fry for 5 more minutes. Shake up and cook for another 3 minutes. Set the veggies aside.
4. On a plate, put the breadcrumbs. In a bowl, whisk chickpea flour and hot sauce. Toss in tofu cubes until coated and dip them in the breadcrumbs.
5. Air Fry tofu for 10 minutes until crispy.
6. Share quinoa and fried veggies into 2 bowls. Top with crispy tofu and drizzle with lemon juice, olive oil and salt to taste.
7. Scatter with scallions and sesame seeds before serving.

Variations & Ingredients Tips:

- Use cauliflower, Brussels sprouts, or carrots instead of broccoli.
- Substitute quinoa with brown rice, farro, or couscous.
- Add avocado slices or hummus for extra creaminess.

Per Serving: Calories: 620; Total Fat: 26g; Saturated Fat: 3.5g; Sodium: 1120mg; Total Carbohydrates: 71g; Dietary Fiber: 11g; Total Sugars: 9g; Protein: 35g

Tofu & Spinach Lasagna

Servings: 4 | Prep Time: 20 Minutes | Cooking Time: 30 Minutes

Ingredients:

- 227 grams cooked lasagne noodles
- 1 tbsp olive oil
- 2 cups crumbled tofu
- 2 cups fresh spinach
- 2 tbsp cornstarch
- 1 tsp onion powder
- Salt and pepper to taste
- 2 garlic cloves, minced
- 2 cups marinara sauce

- ½ cup shredded mozzarella

Directions:

1. Warm the olive oil in a large pan over medium heat. Add the tofu and spinach and stir-fry for a minute. Add the cornstarch, onion powder, salt, pepper, and garlic. Stir until the spinach wilts. Remove from heat.
2. Preheat air fryer to 200°C/390°F.
3. Pour a thin layer of pasta sauce in a baking pan. Layer 2-3 lasagne noodles on top of the marinara sauce. Top with a little more sauce and some of the tofu mix. Add another 2-3 noodles on top, then another layer of sauce, then another layer of tofu. Finish with a layer of noodles and a final layer of sauce. Sprinkle with mozzarella cheese on top.
4. Place the pan in the air fryer and Bake for 15 minutes or until the noodle edges are browned and the cheese is melted.
5. Cut and serve.

Variations & Ingredients Tips:

- Substitute tofu with ricotta cheese for a more traditional lasagna.
- Add sautéed mushrooms, zucchini, or bell peppers to the filling.
- Use gluten-free lasagna noodles for a gluten-free version.

Per Serving: Calories: 420; Total Fat: 15g; Saturated Fat: 4g; Sodium: 720mg; Total Carbohydrates: 53g; Dietary Fiber: 6g; Total Sugars: 9g; Protein: 23g

Stuffed Portobellos

Servings: 4 | Prep Time: 20 Minutes | Cooking Time: 45 Minutes

Ingredients:

- 1 cup cherry tomatoes
- 2 ¼ tsp olive oil
- 3 tbsp grated mozzarella
- 1 cup chopped baby spinach
- 1 garlic clove, minced
- ¼ tsp dried oregano

- ¼ tsp dried thyme
- Salt and pepper to taste
- ¼ cup bread crumbs
- 4 portobello mush-rooms, stemmed and gills removed
- 1 tbsp chopped parsley

Directions:

1. Preheat air fryer to 180°C/360°F.
2. Combine tomatoes, ¼ teaspoon olive oil, and salt in a small bowl. Arrange in a single layer in the parchment-lined air fryer basket and Air Fry for 10 minutes. Stir and flatten the tomatoes with the back of a spoon, then Air Fry for another 6-8 minutes.
3. Transfer the tomatoes to a medium bowl and combine with spinach, garlic, oregano, thyme, pepper, bread crumbs, and the rest of the olive oil.
4. Place the mushrooms on a work surface with the gills facing up. Spoon tomato mixture and mozzarella cheese equally into the mushroom caps and transfer the mushrooms to the air fryer basket.
5. Air Fry for 8-10 minutes until the mushrooms have softened and the tops are golden.
6. Garnish with chopped parsley and serve.

Variations & Ingredients Tips:

- Substitute portobello mushrooms with large button mushrooms or zucchini boats.
- Add cooked quinoa, rice, or ground meat to the filling for a heartier dish.
- Top with a drizzle of balsamic glaze or pesto sauce before serving.

Per Serving: Calories: 130; Total Fat: 7g; Saturated Fat: 2g; Sodium: 200mg; Total Carbohydrates: 12g; Dietary Fiber: 3g; Total Sugars: 4g; Protein: 7g

Powerful Jackfruit Fritters

Servings:4 | Prep Time: 20 Minutes | Cooking Time: 30 Minutes

Ingredients:

- 1 can jackfruit, chopped
- 1 egg, beaten
- 1 tbsp Dijon mustard
- 1 tbsp mayonnaise
- 1 tbsp prepared horseradish
- 2 tbsp grated yellow onion
- 2 tbsp chopped parsley
- 2 tbsp chopped nori
- 2 tbsp flour
- 1 tbsp Cajun seasoning
- ¼ tsp garlic powder
- ¼ tsp salt
- 2 lemon wedges

Directions:

1. In a bowl, combine jackfruit, egg, mustard, mayonnaise, horseradish, onion, parsley, nori, flour, Cajun seasoning, garlic, and salt. Let chill in the fridge for 15 minutes.
2. Preheat air fryer to 180°C/350°F.
3. Divide the mixture into 12 balls. Place them in the air fryer basket and Air Fry for 10 minutes.
4. Serve with lemon wedges.

Variations & Ingredients Tips:

- Substitute jackfruit with canned artichoke hearts or hearts of palm.
- Use Old Bay seasoning instead of Cajun for a different spice profile.
- Serve with tartar sauce or spicy remoulade.

Per Serving: Calories: 120; Total Fat: 5g; Saturated Fat: 1g; Sodium: 730mg; Total Carbohydrates: 16g; Dietary Fiber: 3g; Total Sugars: 6g; Protein: 4g

Breaded Avocado Tacos

Servings: 3 | Prep Time: 15 Minutes | Cooking Time: 20 Minutes

Ingredients:

- 2 tomatoes, diced
- ¼ cup diced red onion
- 1 jalapeño, finely diced
- 1 tbsp lime juice
- 1 tsp lime zest
- ¼ cup chopped cilantro
- 1 tsp salt
- 1 egg
- 2 tbsp milk
- 1 cup breadcrumbs
- ¼ cup almond flour

- 1 avocado, sliced into fries
- 6 flour tortillas
- 1 cup coleslaw mix

Directions:

1. In a bowl, combine the tomatoes, jalapeño, red onion, lime juice, lime zest, cilantro, and salt. Let chill the pico de gallo covered in the fridge until ready to use.
2. Preheat air fryer at 190°C/375°F. In a small bowl, beat egg and milk. In another bowl, add breadcrumbs. Dip avocado slices in the egg mixture, then dredge them in the mixed almond flour and breadcrumbs. Place avocado slices in the greased frying basket and Air Fry for 5 minutes. Add 2 avocado fries to each tortilla. Top each with coleslaw mix. Serve immediately.

Variations & Ingredients Tips:

- Substitute flour tortillas with corn tortillas for a gluten-free option.
- Add shredded cheese, sour cream, or hot sauce for extra toppings.
- Use panko breadcrumbs for a crunchier texture.

Per Serving (2 tacos): Calories: 450; Cholesterol: 65mg; Total Fat: 23g; Saturated Fat: 4g; Sodium: 1020mg; Total Carbohydrates: 53g; Dietary Fiber: 8g; Total Sugars: 6g; Protein: 12g

Thai Peanut Veggie Burgers

Servings: 6 | Prep Time: 20 Minutes | Cooking Time: 14 Minutes

Ingredients:

- One 440-gram can cannellini beans
- 1 teaspoon minced garlic
- ¼ cup chopped onion
- 1 Thai chili pepper, sliced
- 2 tablespoons natural peanut butter
- ½ teaspoon black pepper
- ½ teaspoon salt
- ⅓ cup all-purpose flour (optional)
- ½ cup cooked quinoa
- 1 large carrot, grated
- 1 cup shredded red cabbage
- ¼ cup peanut dressing
- ¼ cup chopped cilantro
- 6 Hawaiian rolls
- 6 butterleaf lettuce leaves

Directions:

1. Preheat the air fryer to 180°C/350°F.
2. To a blender or food processor fitted with a metal blade, add the beans, garlic, onion, chili pepper, peanut butter, pepper, and salt. Pulse for 5 to 10 seconds. Do not over process. The mixture should be coarse, not smooth.
3. Remove from the blender or food processor and spoon into a large bowl. Mix in the cooked quinoa and carrots. At this point, the mixture should begin to hold together to form small patties. If the dough appears to be too sticky (meaning you likely processed a little too long), add the flour to hold the patties together.
4. Using a large spoon, form 8 equal patties out of the batter.
5. Liberally spray a metal trivet with olive oil spray and set in the air fryer basket. Place the patties into the basket, leaving enough space to be able to turn them with a spatula.
6. Cook for 7 minutes, flip, and cook another 7 minutes.
7. Remove from the heat and repeat with additional patties.
8. To serve, place the red cabbage in a bowl and toss with peanut dressing and cilantro. Place the veggie burger on a bun, and top with a slice of lettuce and cabbage slaw.

Variations & Ingredients Tips:

- Use chickpeas or black beans instead of cannellini beans.
- Substitute peanut butter with almond butter or sunflower seed butter.
- Add shredded beetroot or zucchini to the patty mixture.

Per Serving: Calories: 340; Total Fat: 11g; Saturated Fat: 2g; Sodium: 580mg; Total Carbohydrates: 50g; Dietary Fiber: 9g; Total Sugars: 8g; Protein: 13g

Thyme Meatless Patties

Ingredients:

- ½ cup oat flour
- 1 tsp allspice
- ½ tsp ground thyme
- 1 tsp maple syrup
- ½ tsp liquid smoke
- 1 tsp balsamic vinegar

Directions:

1. Preheat air fryer to 200°C/400°F.
2. Mix the oat flour, allspice, thyme, maple syrup, liquid smoke, balsamic vinegar, and 2 tbsp of water in a bowl.
3. Make 6 patties out of the mixture. Place them onto a parchment paper and flatten them to 1-cm thick. Grease the patties with cooking spray.
4. Grill for 12 minutes until crispy, turning once.
5. Serve warm.

Variations & Ingredients Tips:

- Add finely chopped walnuts, sunflower seeds, or pumpkin seeds for crunch.
- Use date syrup or agave nectar instead of maple syrup.
- Serve with a dipping sauce like BBQ, ketchup, or sweet chili sauce.

Per Serving: Calories: 110; Total Fat: 2g; Saturated Fat: 0g; Sodium: 5mg; Total Carbohydrates: 19g; Dietary Fiber: 2g; Total Sugars: 4g; Protein: 3g

Fried Potatoes With Bell Peppers

Ingredients:

- 3 russet potatoes, cubed
- 1 tbsp canola oil
- 1 tbsp olive oil
- 1 tsp paprika
- Salt and pepper to taste
- 1 chopped shallot
- 1/2 chopped red bell pepper
- 1/2 diced yellow bell pepper

Directions:

1. Preheat air fryer to 190°C/370°F.
2. Whisk the canola oil, olive oil, paprika, salt, and pepper in a bowl. Toss in the potatoes to coat.
3. Place the potatoes in the air fryer and Bake for 20 minutes, shaking the basket periodically.
4. Top the potatoes with shallot and bell peppers and cook for an additional 3-4 minutes or until the potatoes are cooked through and the peppers are soft.
5. Serve warm.

Variations & Ingredients Tips:

- Add smoked paprika or cayenne for a spicy kick.
- Toss in fresh herbs like rosemary or thyme before serving.
- Top with vegan cheese shreds for extra richness.

Per Serving: Calories: 220; Total Fat: 9g; Saturated Fat: 1g; Sodium: 110mg; Total Carbs: 32g; Dietary Fiber: 4g; Total Sugars: 3g; Protein: 4g

Crispy Apple Fries With Caramel Sauce

Ingredients:

- 4 medium apples, cored
- ¼ tsp cinnamon
- ¼ tsp nutmeg
- 1 cup caramel sauce

Directions:

1. Preheat air fryer to 175°C/350°F. Slice the apples to a 8-mm thickness for a crunchy chip. Place in a large bowl and sprinkle with cinnamon and nutmeg. Place the slices in the air

fryer basket. Bake for 6 minutes. Shake the basket, then cook for another 4 minutes or until crunchy. Serve drizzled with caramel sauce and enjoy!

Variations & Ingredients Tips:

- Use different apple varieties like Granny Smith, Honeycrisp, or Fuji for varied flavors.
- Substitute caramel sauce with melted chocolate or peanut butter for a different dip.
- Sprinkle with chopped nuts or granola for extra crunch.

Per Serving: Calories: 310; Cholesterol: 15mg; Total Fat: 6g; Saturated Fat: 3.5g; Sodium: 260mg; Total Carbohydrates: 64g; Dietary Fiber: 5g; Total Sugars: 51g; Protein: 1g

Fennel Tofu Bites

Servings: 4 | Prep Time: 10 Minutes | Cooking Time: 35 Minutes

Ingredients:

- 1/3 cup vegetable broth
- 2 tbsp tomato sauce
- 2 tsp soy sauce
- 1 tbsp nutritional yeast
- 1 tsp Italian seasoning
- 1 tsp granulated sugar
- 1 tsp grated ginger
- 1/2 tsp fennel seeds
- 1/2 tsp garlic pow-

- der
- Salt and pepper to taste
- 400g firm tofu, cubed
- 2/3 cup breadcrumbs
- 1 tsp Italian seasoning
- 2 tsp toasted sesame seeds
- 1 cup warm marinara sauce

Directions:

1. In a large bowl, whisk the vegetable broth, soy sauce, ginger, tomato sauce, nutritional yeast, Italian seasoning, sugar, fennel seeds, garlic powder, salt and black pepper. Toss in tofu to coat. Let marinate covered in the fridge for 30 minutes, tossing once.
2. Preheat air fryer at 175°C/350°F. Mix the breadcrumbs, Italian seasoning, and salt in a

bowl. Strain marinade from tofu cubes and dredge them in the breadcrumb mixture.
3. Place tofu cubes in the greased frying basket and Air Fry for 10 minutes, turning once.
4. Serve sprinkled with sesame seeds and marinara sauce on the side.

Variations & Ingredients Tips:

- Use panko breadcrumbs for an extra crispy coating.
- Add red pepper flakes to the marinade for a spicy kick.
- Make it gluten-free by using gluten-free breadcrumbs.

Per Serving: Calories: 240; Total Fat: 9g; Saturated Fat: 1.5g; Sodium: 400mg; Total Carbs: 28g; Dietary Fiber: 4g; Total Sugars: 5g; Protein: 14g

Basil Green Beans

Servings: 4 | Prep Time: 5 Minutes | Cooking Time: 15 Minutes

Ingredients:

- 680 grams green beans, trimmed
- 1 tbsp olive oil
- 1 tbsp fresh basil, chopped
- Garlic salt to taste

Directions:

1. Preheat air fryer to 200°C/400°F. Coat the green beans with olive oil in a large bowl. Combine with fresh basil and garlic salt. Put the beans in the frying basket and Air Fry for 7-9 minutes, shaking once until the beans begin to brown. Serve warm and enjoy!

Variations & Ingredients Tips:

- Add sliced almonds or chopped bacon for extra crunch and flavor.
- Substitute basil with other fresh herbs like parsley, thyme, or oregano.
- Drizzle with balsamic vinegar or lemon juice before serving for a tangy twist.

Per Serving: Calories: 70; Cholesterol: 0mg; Total Fat: 4g; Saturated Fat: 0.5g; Sodium: 75mg;

Total Carbohydrates: 9g; Dietary Fiber: 4g; Total   Sugars: 4g; Protein: 2g

Vegetable Side Dishes Recipes

Greek-inspired Ratatouille

Servings: 6 | Prep Time: 15 Minutes | Cooking Time: 40 Minutes

Ingredients:

- 1 cup cherry tomatoes
- 1/2 bulb fennel, finely sliced
- 2 russet potatoes, cubed
- 1/2 cup tomatoes, cubed
- 1 eggplant, cubed
- 1 zucchini, cubed
- 1 red onion, chopped
- 1 red bell pepper, chopped
- 2 garlic cloves, minced
- 1 tsp dried mint
- 1 tsp dried parsley
- 1 tsp dried oregano
- Salt and pepper to taste
- 1/4 tsp red pepper flakes
- 1/3 cup olive oil
- 1 can tomato paste
- 1/4 cup vegetable broth

Directions:

1. Preheat air fryer to 160°C/320°F.
2. Mix the potatoes, tomatoes, fennel, eggplant, zucchini, onion, bell pepper, garlic, mint, parsley, oregano, salt, black pepper, and red pepper flakes in a bowl.
3. Whisk the olive oil, tomato paste, broth, and 1/4 cup of water in a small bowl. Toss the mixture with the vegetables.
4. Pour the coated vegetables into the air frying basket in a single layer and roast for 20 minutes.
5. Stir well and spread out again. Roast for an additional 10 minutes, then repeat the process and cook for another 10 minutes.
6. Serve and enjoy!

Variations & Ingredients Tips:

- Add chickpeas or white beans for extra protein.
- Swap zucchini for yellow squash.
- Use fresh herbs instead of dried.

Per Serving: Calories: 210; Total Fat: 14g; Saturated Fat: 2g; Cholesterol: 0mg; Sodium: 120mg; Total Carbohydrates: 21g; Dietary Fiber: 5g; Total Sugars: 8g; Protein: 3g

Hasselback Garlic-and-butter Potatoes

Servings: 3 | Prep Time: 10 Minutes | Cooking Time: 48 Minutes

Ingredients:

- 3 (227g) russet potatoes
- 6 brown button or baby bella mushrooms, very thinly sliced
- Olive oil spray
- 3 tablespoons butter, melted and
- cooled
- 1 tablespoon minced garlic
- 3/4 teaspoon table salt
- 3 tablespoons (about 14g) finely grated Parmesan cheese

Directions:

1. Preheat the air fryer to 180°C/350°F.
2. Cut slits down the length of each potato, about three-quarters down into the potato and spaced about 6mm apart. Wedge a thin mushroom slice in each slit. Generously coat the potatoes on all sides with olive oil spray.
3. When the machine is at temperature, set the po-

tatoes mushroom side up in the basket with as much air space between them as possible. Air-fry undisturbed for 45 minutes, or tender when pricked with a fork.

4. Increase the machine's temperature to 200°C/400°F. Use kitchen tongs, and perhaps a flatware fork for balance, to gently transfer the potatoes to a cutting board. Brush each evenly with butter, then sprinkle the minced garlic and salt over them. Sprinkle the cheese evenly over the potatoes.

5. Use those same tongs to gently transfer the potatoes cheese side up to the basket in one layer with some space for air flow between them. Air-fry undisturbed for 3 minutes, or until the cheese has melted and begun to brown.

6. Use those same tongs to gently transfer the potatoes back to the wire rack. Cool for 5 minutes before serving.

Variations & Ingredients Tips:

● Use sweet potatoes instead of russets.
● Mix herbs like rosemary or thyme into the melted butter.
● Top with crispy bacon bits after baking.

Per Serving: Calories: 280; Total Fat: 16g; Saturated Fat: 8g; Cholesterol: 35mg; Sodium: 650mg; Total Carbohydrates: 32g; Dietary Fiber: 3g; Total Sugars: 1g; Protein: 6g

Hot Okra Wedges

Servings: 2 | Prep Time: 10 Minutes | Cooking Time: 35 Minutes

Ingredients:

● 237g okra, sliced
● 1 cup breadcrumbs
● 2 eggs, beaten
● A pinch of black pepper
● 1 tsp crushed red peppers
● 2 tsp hot Tabasco sauce

Directions:

1. Preheat air fryer to 180°C/350°F.
2. Place the eggs and Tabasco sauce in a bowl and stir thoroughly; set aside.

3. In a separate bowl, combine the breadcrumbs, crushed red peppers, and black pepper.
4. Dip the okra into the beaten eggs, then coat in the crumb mixture.
5. Lay the okra pieces on the greased frying basket.
6. Air fry for 14-16 minutes, shaking basket several times during cooking until crispy and golden brown.
7. Serve.

Variations & Ingredients Tips:

● Use panko breadcrumbs for extra crunch.
● Substitute hot sauce for a Cajun seasoning blend.
● Serve with a cool ranch dipping sauce.

Per Serving: Calories: 258; Total Fat: 5g; Saturated Fat: 1g; Cholesterol: 107mg; Sodium: 515mg; Total Carbs: 45g; Dietary Fiber: 5g; Total Sugars: 4g; Protein: 10g

Onions

Servings: 4 | Prep Time: 5 Minutes | Cooking Time: 18 Minutes

Ingredients:

● 2 yellow onions (Vidalia or 1015 recommended)
● Salt and pepper
● 1/4 teaspoon ground thyme
● 1/4 teaspoon smoked paprika
● 2 teaspoons olive oil
● 28g Gruyère cheese, grated

Directions:

1. Peel onions and halve lengthwise (vertically).
2. Sprinkle cut sides of onions with salt, pepper, thyme, and paprika.
3. Place each onion half, cut-surface up, on a large square of aluminum foil. Pull sides of foil up to cup around onion. Drizzle cut surface of onions with oil.
4. Crimp foil at top to seal closed.
5. Place wrapped onions in air fryer basket and cook at 199°C/390°F for 18 minutes. When done, onions should be soft enough to pierce

with fork but still slightly firm.

6. Open foil just enough to sprinkle each onion with grated cheese.
7. Cook for 30 seconds to 1 minute to melt cheese.

Variations & Ingredients Tips:

● Use sweet or red onions instead of yellow.
● Mix grated cheese with breadcrumbs before topping for a crispy crust.
● Add a pat of butter to the center before wrapping for extra richness.

Per Serving: Calories: 93; Total Fat: 5g; Saturated Fat: 2g; Cholesterol: 5mg; Sodium: 86mg; Total Carbohydrates: 11g; Dietary Fiber: 2g; Total Sugars: 5g; Protein: 3g

Tasty Brussels Sprouts With Guanciale

Servings: 4 | Prep Time: 10 Minutes | Cooking Time: 50 Minutes

Ingredients:

● 3 guanciale slices, halved
● 450 g Brussels sprouts, halved
● 2 tablespoons olive
oil
● ¼ teaspoon salt
● ¼ teaspoon dried thyme

Directions:

1. Preheat air fryer to 180°C/350°F.
2. Lay the guanciale in the air fryer, until crispy, 10 minutes. Remove and drain on a paper towel. Give the guanciale a rough chop and set aside.
3. Coat Brussels sprouts with olive oil in a large bowl. Add salt and thyme, then toss.
4. Place the sprouts in the frying basket. Air Fry for about 12-15 minutes, shake the basket once until the sprouts are golden and tender.
5. Top with guanciale and serve.

Variations & Ingredients Tips:

● Use bacon or pancetta instead of guanciale for

a different flavor profile.
● Add some minced garlic or red pepper flakes to the Brussels sprouts for extra flavor.
● Serve the Brussels sprouts with a dipping sauce, such as honey mustard or balsamic glaze.

Per Serving: Calories: 160; Total Fat: 12g; Saturated Fat: 3.5g; Cholesterol: 15mg; Sodium: 320mg; Total Carbs: 8g; Fiber: 3g; Sugars: 2g; Protein: 6g

Fried Pearl Onions With Balsamic Vinegar And Basil

Servings: 2 | Prep Time: 5 Minutes | Cooking Time: 10 Minutes

Ingredients:

● 454g fresh pearl onions
● 1 tablespoon olive oil
● Salt and freshly ground black pepper
● 1 teaspoon high quality aged balsamic vinegar
● 1 tablespoon chopped fresh basil leaves (or mint)

Directions:

1. Preheat air fryer to 200°C/400°F.
2. Decide to peel onions before or after cooking. Trim root ends if peeling first.
3. Toss pearl onions with olive oil, salt and pepper.
4. Air fry for 10 minutes, shaking basket a couple times during cooking. Add 2-3 mins for larger onions.
5. Let onions cool slightly and slip off any remaining skins.
6. Toss onions with balsamic vinegar and basil.
7. Serve.

Variations & Ingredients Tips:

● Use shallots instead of pearl onions.
● Add a pinch of red pepper flakes for heat.
● Substitute fresh thyme or parsley for the basil.

Per Serving: Calories: 135; Total Fat: 6g; Saturated Fat: 1g; Cholesterol: 0mg; Sodium: 10mg; Total Carbs: 18g; Fiber: 3g; Sugars: 6g; Protein: 2g

Toasted Choco-nuts

Servings: 2 | Prep Time: 5 Minutes | Cooking Time: 10 Minutes

Ingredients:

- 2 cups almonds
- 2 teaspoons maple syrup
- 2 tablespoons cacao powder

Directions:

1. Preheat air fryer to 180°C/350°F.
2. Distribute the almonds in a single layer in the frying basket and Bake for 3 minutes.
3. Shake the basket and Bake for another 1 minute until golden brown.
4. Remove them to a bowl. Drizzle with maple syrup and toss.
5. Sprinkle with cacao powder and toss until well coated.
6. Let cool completely.
7. Store in a container at room temperature for up to 2 weeks or in the fridge for up to a month.

Variations & Ingredients Tips:

- Use different types of nuts, such as cashews or pecans, for a variety of flavors and textures.
- Add some ground cinnamon or vanilla extract for extra flavor.
- For a savory version, replace the maple syrup and cacao powder with olive oil and your favorite spice blend.

Per Serving: Calories: 580; Total Fat: 51g; Saturated Fat: 4g; Cholesterol: 0mg; Sodium: 0mg; Total Carbs: 27g; Fiber: 13g; Sugars: 9g; Protein: 21g

Buttery Rolls

Servings: 6 Rolls | Prep Time: 15 Minutes

| Cooking Time: 14 Minutes

Ingredients:

- 6½ tablespoons Room-temperature whole or low-fat milk
- 3 tablespoons plus 1 teaspoon Butter, melted and cooled
- 3 tablespoons plus 1 teaspoon (or 1 medium egg, well beaten) Pasteurized egg substitute, such as Egg Beaters
- 1½ tablespoons Granulated white sugar
- 1¼ teaspoons Instant yeast
- ¼ teaspoon Table salt
- 2 cups, plus more for dusting All-purpose flour
- Vegetable oil
- Additional melted butter, for brushing

Directions:

1. Stir the milk, melted butter, pasteurized egg substitute (or whole egg), sugar, yeast, and salt in a medium bowl to combine. Stir in the flour just until the mixture makes a soft dough.
2. Lightly flour a clean, dry work surface. Turn the dough out onto the work surface. Knead the dough for 5 minutes to develop the gluten.
3. Lightly oil the inside of a clean medium bowl. Gather the dough into a compact ball and set it in the bowl. Turn the dough over so that its surface has oil on it all over. Cover the bowl tightly with plastic wrap and set aside in a warm, draft-free place until the dough has doubled in bulk, about 1½ hours.
4. Punch down the dough, then turn it out onto a clean, dry work surface. Divide it into 5 even balls for a small batch, 6 balls for a medium batch, or 8 balls for a large one.
5. For a small batch, lightly oil the inside of a 15cm round cake pan and set the balls around its perimeter, separating them as much as possible. For a medium batch, lightly oil the inside of a 18cm round cake pan and set the balls in it with one ball at its center, separating them as much as possible. For a large batch, lightly oil the inside of a 20cm round cake pan and set the balls in it with one at the center, separating them as much as possible.
6. Cover with plastic wrap and set aside to rise for

30 minutes.

7. Preheat the air fryer to 177°C/350°F.

8. Uncover the pan and brush the rolls with a little melted butter, perhaps ½ teaspoon per roll. When the machine is at temperature, set the cake pan in the basket. Air-fry undisturbed for 14 minutes, or until the rolls have risen and browned.

9. Using kitchen tongs and a nonstick-safe spatula, two hot pads, or silicone baking mitts, transfer the cake pan from the basket to a wire rack. Cool the rolls in the pan for a minute or two. Turn the rolls out onto a wire rack, set them top side up again, and cool for at least another couple of minutes before serving warm.

Variations & Ingredients Tips:

● Add grated cheese or herbs to the dough before kneading.

● Brush with garlic butter or herb butter instead of plain melted butter.

● Serve with flavored butters like honey butter or cinnamon butter.

Per Serving (1 roll): Calories: 200; Total Fat: 6g; Saturated Fat: 3g; Cholesterol: 15mg; Sodium: 150mg; Total Carbs: 32g; Fiber: 1g; Sugars: 3g; Protein: 5g

Spiced Roasted Acorn Squash

Servings: 2 | Prep Time: 5 Minutes | Cooking Time: 45 Minutes

Ingredients:

● ½ acorn squash half
● 1 teaspoon butter, melted
● 2 teaspoons light brown sugar
● ⅛ teaspoon ground cinnamon
● 2 tablespoons hot sauce
● 60 ml maple syrup

Directions:

1. Preheat air fryer at 200°C/400°F.

2. Slice off about 6 mm from the side of the squash half to sit flat like a bowl.

3. In a bowl, combine all ingredients. Brush over the top of the squash and pour any remaining mixture in the middle of the squash.

4. Place squash in the frying basket and Roast for 35 minutes.

5. Cut it in half and divide between 2 serving plates. Serve.

Variations & Ingredients Tips:

● Try using different types of winter squash, such as butternut squash or pumpkin, for a variety of flavors.

● Add some chopped nuts, such as pecans or walnuts, for a crunchy texture.

● For a savory version, replace the brown sugar and cinnamon with garlic powder, thyme, and Parmesan cheese.

Per Serving: Calories: 190; Total Fat: 3g; Saturated Fat: 2g; Cholesterol: 5mg; Sodium: 450mg; Total Carbs: 40g; Fiber: 2g; Sugars: 30g; Protein: 1g

Stuffed Avocados

Servings: 4 | Prep Time: 10 Minutes | Cooking Time: 8 Minutes

Ingredients:

● 1 cup frozen shoepeg corn, thawed
● 1 cup cooked black beans
● ¼ cup diced onion
● ½ teaspoon cumin
● 2 teaspoons lime juice, plus extra for serving
● Salt and pepper
● 2 large avocados, split in half, pit removed

Directions:

1. Mix together the corn, beans, onion, cumin, and lime juice. Season to taste with salt and pepper.

2. Scoop out some of the flesh from center of each avocado and set aside. Divide corn mixture evenly between the cavities.

3. Set avocado halves in air fryer basket and cook at 180°C/360°F for 8 minutes, until corn mixture is hot.

4. Season the avocado flesh that you scooped out with a squirt of lime juice, salt, and pepper. Spoon it over the cooked halves.

Variations & Ingredients Tips:

● Add some diced jalapeño or red pepper flakes for a spicy kick.
● Use different types of beans, such as kidney beans or pinto beans, for a variety of flavors and textures.
● Top the stuffed avocados with some shredded cheese, sour cream, or salsa for extra flavor.

Per Serving: Calories: 230; Total Fat: 16g; Saturated Fat: 2g; Cholesterol: 0mg; Sodium: 120mg; Total Carbs: 21g; Fiber: 10g; Sugars: 2g; Protein: 6g

Roasted Herbed Shiitake Mushrooms

Cooking Time: 5 Minutes | Prep Time: 5 Minutes | Servings: 4

Ingredients:

● 227g shiitake mushrooms, stemmed and caps chopped
● 1 tablespoon olive oil
● 1/2 teaspoon salt
● Freshly ground black pepper
● 1 teaspoon chopped fresh thyme
● 1 teaspoon chopped fresh oregano
● 1 tablespoon chopped fresh parsley

Directions:

1. Preheat air fryer to 200°C/400°F.
2. In a bowl, toss mushrooms with olive oil, salt, pepper, thyme and oregano.
3. Transfer mushrooms to air fryer basket and cook for 5 minutes, shaking basket 1-2 times.
4. For more tender mushrooms, increase cook time by 2 minutes.
5. Once cooked, toss mushrooms with chopped parsley.
6. Season again to taste and serve.

Variations & Ingredients Tips:

● Use a blend of wild mushroom varieties.
● Add minced garlic or shallots before roasting.
● Finish with a squeeze of lemon juice.

Per Serving: Calories: 55; Total Fat: 4g; Saturated Fat: 1g; Cholesterol: 0mg; Sodium: 234mg; Total Carbohydrates: 4g; Dietary Fiber: 1g; Total Sugars: 2g; Protein: 2g

Fried Corn On The Cob

Servings: 2 | Prep Time: 10 Minutes | Cooking Time: 10 Minutes

Ingredients:

● 1 ½ tablespoons Regular or low-fat mayonnaise
● 1 ½ teaspoons Minced garlic
● ¼ teaspoon Table salt
● ¾ cup Plain panko bread crumbs
● 3 10cm lengths husked and de-silked corn on the cob
● Vegetable oil spray

Directions:

1. Preheat air fryer to 200°C/400°F.
2. Stir mayo, garlic, salt. Spread panko on a plate.
3. Brush mayo mix over corn kernels. Roll in panko to coat.
4. Spray corn with oil. Set aside and coat remaining pieces.
5. Set coated corn in basket with space between. Air fry 10 mins until crisp.
6. Transfer to wire rack. Cool 5 mins before serving.

Variations & Ingredients Tips:

● Use chipotle mayo for a smoky flavor.
● Add parmesan or cajun seasoning to the breadcrumb coating.
● Serve with lime wedges for squeezing over.

Per Serving: Calories: 210; Total Fat: 8g; Saturated Fat: 1g; Cholesterol: 5mg; Sodium: 440mg; Total Carbs: 31g; Fiber: 3g; Sugars: 3g; Protein: 6g

Green Peas With Mint

Servings: 4 | Prep Time: 5 Minutes | Cooking Time: 5 Minutes

Ingredients:

- 1 cup shredded lettuce
- 284g package frozen green peas, thawed
- 1 tablespoon fresh mint, shredded
- 1 teaspoon melted butter

Directions:

1. Lay the shredded lettuce in the air fryer basket.
2. Toss together the peas, mint, and melted butter and spoon over the lettuce.
3. Cook at 180°C/360°F for 5 minutes, until peas are warm and lettuce wilts.

Variations & Ingredients Tips:

- Add lemon zest or juice for extra brightness.
- Use olive oil instead of butter.
- Mix in crumbled feta or goat cheese.

Per Serving: Calories: 80; Total Fat: 1.5g; Saturated Fat: 0.5g; Cholesterol: 0mg; Sodium: 65mg; Total Carbohydrates: 12g; Dietary Fiber: 4g; Total Sugars: 5g; Protein: 5g

Rich Baked Sweet Potatoes

Servings: 2 | Prep Time: 5 Minutes | Cooking Time: 55 Minutes

Ingredients:

- 454g sweet potatoes, scrubbed and perforated with a fork
- 2 tsp olive oil
- Salt and pepper to taste
- 2 tbsp butter
- 3 tbsp honey

Directions:

1. Preheat air fryer at 205°C/400°F.
2. Mix olive oil, salt, pepper and honey in a bowl.
3. Brush the sweet potatoes all over with the honey oil mixture.
4. Place sweet potatoes in the air fryer basket and bake for 45 minutes, turning over halfway.
5. Let cool 10 minutes until cool enough to handle.
6. Slice each potato lengthwise and press ends together to open up slices.
7. Top with butter before serving.

Variations & Ingredients Tips:

- Add cinnamon, nutmeg or pumpkin spice to the honey oil mixture.
- Stuff baked sweet potatoes with sauteed spinach or black beans.
- Top with pecans, marshmallows or brown sugar before serving.

Per Serving: Calories: 291; Total Fat: 11g; Saturated Fat: 4g; Cholesterol: 15mg; Sodium: 115mg; Total Carbohydrates: 48g; Dietary Fiber: 5g; Total Sugars: 23g; Protein: 2g

Perfect French Fries

Servings: 3 | Prep Time: 10 Minutes | Cooking Time: 37 Minutes

Ingredients:

- 454g large russet potatoes
- Vegetable oil or olive oil spray
- 1/2 teaspoon table salt

Directions:

1. Cut each potato lengthwise into 6mm thick slices, then cut each slice into 6mm thick fry strips.
2. Soak the fry strips in cool water for 5 minutes. Drain and pat very dry with paper towels.
3. Preheat air fryer to 110°C/225°F.
4. Arrange fries in an even layer in the basket and air fry for 20 minutes, tossing twice.
5. Transfer fries to a bowl. Increase air fryer temperature to 160°C/325°F.
6. Generously coat fries with oil spray, tossing several times to evenly coat all over.
7. When air fryer is at temp, return fries to basket and air fry 12 minutes, tossing twice.
8. Increase temperature to 190°C/375°F. Air fry 5

more minutes, tossing frequently, until browned and crispy.

9. Transfer to a bowl, toss with salt, and serve hot.

Variations & Ingredients Tips:

- Cut fries into thin shoestring or thicker steak fry shapes.
- Toss with cajun seasoning, ranch powder or grated parmesan.
- Serve with ketchup, ranch, cheese sauce or chili for dipping/topping.

Per Serving: Calories: 189; Total Fat: 0g; Saturated Fat: 0g; Cholesterol: 0mg; Sodium: 147mg; Total Carbohydrates: 42g; Dietary Fiber: 3g; Total Sugars: 2g; Protein: 4g

---

Beet Fries

Servings: 3 | Prep Time: 10 Minutes | Cooking Time: 22 Minutes

Ingredients:

- 3 170g red beets
- Vegetable oil spray
- To taste Coarse sea salt or kosher salt

Directions:

1. Preheat the air fryer to 190°C/375°F.
2. Remove the stems from the beets and peel them with a knife or vegetable peeler. Slice them into 1.3cm-thick circles. Lay these flat on a cutting board and slice them into 1.3cm-thick sticks. Generously coat the sticks on all sides with vegetable oil spray.
3. When the machine is at temperature, drop them into the basket, shake the basket to even the sticks out into as close to one layer as possible, and air-fry for 20 minutes, tossing and rearranging the beet matchsticks every 5 minutes, or until brown and even crisp at the ends. If the machine is at 182°C/360°F, you may need to add 2 minutes to the cooking time.
4. Pour the fries into a big bowl, add the salt, toss well, and serve warm.

Variations & Ingredients Tips:

- Toss with smoked paprika and fresh parsley after cooking.
- Add a squeeze of lemon juice and zest for brightness.
- Serve with a creamy dill or lemon aioli for dipping.

Per Serving: Calories: 70; Total Fat: 0g; Saturated Fat: 0g; Cholesterol: 0mg; Sodium: 170mg; Total Carbs: 16g; Fiber: 4g; Sugars: 11g; Protein: 3g

---

Cinnamon Roasted Pumpkin

Servings: 2 | Prep Time: 5 Minutes | Cooking Time: 25 Minutes

Ingredients:

- 454g pumpkin, halved crosswise and seeded
- 1 tsp coconut oil
- 1 tsp sugar
- ½ tsp ground nutmeg
- 1 tsp ground cinnamon

Directions:

1. Prepare the pumpkin by rubbing coconut oil on the cut sides.
2. In a small bowl, combine sugar, nutmeg and cinnamon. Sprinkle over the pumpkin.
3. Preheat air fryer to 163°C/325°F.
4. Put the pumpkin in the greased frying basket, cut sides up.
5. Bake until the squash is soft in the center, 15 minutes. Test with a knife to ensure softness.
6. Serve.

Variations & Ingredients Tips:

- Use maple syrup instead of sugar.
- Add a pinch of ground cloves or ginger.
- Drizzle with honey or sprinkle with pecans after cooking.

Per Serving: Calories: 105; Total Fat: 2g; Saturated Fat: 1g; Cholesterol: 0mg; Sodium: 10mg; Total Carbs: 23g; Fiber: 4g; Sugars: 8g; Protein: 2g

Dauphinoise (potatoes Au Gratin)

Servings: 4 | Prep Time: 15 Minutes | Cooking Time: 30 Minutes

Ingredients:

- ½ cup grated cheddar cheese
- 3 peeled potatoes, sliced
- ½ cup milk
- ½ cup heavy cream
- Salt and pepper to taste
- 1 tsp ground nutmeg

Directions:

1. Preheat air fryer to 177°C/350°F.
2. Place the milk, heavy cream, salt, pepper, and nutmeg in a bowl and mix well.
3. Dip in the potato slices and arrange on a baking dish.
4. Spoon the remaining milk mixture over the potatoes.
5. Scatter the grated cheddar cheese on top.
6. Place the baking dish in the air fryer and Bake for 20 minutes.
7. Serve warm.

Variations & Ingredients Tips:

- Use a mix of cheddar and gruyere or parmesan cheeses.
- Add thinly sliced onions or garlic between the potato layers.
- Substitute half-and-half for the cream to reduce calories.

Per Serving: Calories: 370; Total Fat: 25g; Saturated Fat: 15g; Cholesterol: 80mg; Sodium: 230mg; Total Carbs: 27g; Fiber: 2g; Sugars: 3g; Protein: 10g

Roast Sweet Potatoes With Parmesan

Servings: 4 | Prep Time: 10 Minutes | Cooking Time: 30 Minutes

Ingredients:

- 2 sweet potatoes, peeled and sliced
- 1/4 cup grated Parmesan
- 1 tsp olive oil
- 1 tbsp balsamic vinegar
- 1 tsp dried rosemary

Directions:

1. Preheat air fryer to 204°C/400°F.
2. Place the sweet potato slices and olive oil in a bowl and toss to coat.
3. Spritz with balsamic vinegar and sprinkle with rosemary. Toss again to coat evenly.
4. Transfer sweet potatoes to the air fryer basket in a single layer.
5. Roast for 18-25 minutes, shaking the basket at least once, until potatoes are tender.
6. Sprinkle with Parmesan cheese and serve warm.

Variations & Ingredients Tips:

- Add minced garlic or shallots to the potato coating.
- Use fresh rosemary instead of dried.
- Drizzle with honey or maple syrup before serving.

Per Serving: Calories: 366; Total Fat: 20g; Saturated Fat: 11g; Cholesterol: 89mg; Sodium: 584mg; Total Carbohydrates: 30g; Dietary Fiber: 4g; Total Sugars: 7g; Protein: 21g

Vegetable Roast

Servings: 6 | Prep Time: 10 Minutes | Cooking Time: 20 Minutes

Ingredients:

- 2 tbsp dill, chopped
- 2 zucchini, cubed
- 1 red bell pepper, diced
- 2 garlic cloves,
- sliced
- 2 tbsp olive oil
- ½ tsp salt
- ½ tsp red pepper flakes

Directions:

1. Preheat air fryer to 190°C/380°F. Combine the

zucchini, bell pepper, red pepper flakes, dill and garlic with olive oil and salt in a bowl. Pour the mixture into the frying basket and roast for 14-16 minutes, shaking once. Serve warm.

Variations & Ingredients Tips:

● Add other vegetables like eggplant, mushrooms, or onions for variety.

● Toss with grated Parmesan cheese or crumbled feta before serving for a cheesy twist.

● Serve over quinoa, couscous, or pasta for a heartier dish.

Per Serving: Calories: 67; Total Fat: 5g; Saturated Fat: 1g; Sodium: 199mg; Total Carbohydrates: 5g; Dietary Fiber: 1g; Total Sugars: 3g; Protein: 1g

Desserts And Sweets

Rich Blueberry Biscuit Shortcakes

Servings: 4 | Prep Time: 20 Minutes | Cooking Time: 35 Minutes

Ingredients:

- 450-g blueberries, halved
- 1/4 cup granulated sugar
- 1 tsp orange zest
- 1 cup heavy cream
- 1 tbsp orange juice
- 2 tbsp powdered sugar
- 1/4 tsp cinnamon
- 1/4 tsp nutmeg
- 2 cups flour
- 1 egg yolk
- 1 tbsp baking powder
- 1/2 tsp baking soda
- 1/2 tsp cornstarch
- 1/2 tsp salt
- 1/2 tsp vanilla extract
- 1/2 tsp honey
- 4 tbsp cold butter, cubed
- 1 1/4 cups buttermilk

Directions:

1. Combine blueberries, granulated sugar, and orange zest in a bowl. Let chill the topping covered in the fridge until ready to use.

2. Beat heavy cream, orange juice, egg yolk, vanilla extract and powdered sugar in a metal bowl until peaks form. Let chill the whipped cream covered in the fridge until ready to use.

3. Preheat air fryer at 175°C/350°F.

4. Combine flour, cinnamon, nutmeg, baking powder, baking soda, cornstarch, honey, butter cubes, and buttermilk in a bowl until a sticky dough forms.

5. Flour your hands and form dough into 8 balls. Place them on a lightly greased pizza pan. Place pizza pan in the frying basket and Air Fry for 8 minutes.

6. Transfer biscuits to serving plates and cut them in half. Spread blueberry mixture to each biscuit bottom and place tops of biscuits. Garnish with whipped cream and serve.

Variations & Ingredients Tips:

● Use other berries like raspberries or strawberries instead of blueberries.

● Add lemon or lime zest to the whipped cream for extra flavor.

● Brush the biscuit tops with melted butter before baking.

Per Serving: Calories: 580; Total Fat: 33g; Saturated Fat: 20g; Cholesterol: 135mg; Sodium: 720mg; Total Carbs: 62g; Dietary Fiber: 2g; Total Sugars: 18g; Protein: 9g

Apple & Blueberry Crumble

Servings: 4 | Prep Time: 15 Minutes | Cooking Time: 20 Minutes

Ingredients:

- 5 apples, peeled and diced
- 1/2 lemon, zested and juiced
- 1/2 cup blueberries
- 1 cup brown sugar
- 1 tsp cinnamon
- 1/2 cup butter
- 1/2 cup flour

Directions:

1. Preheat air fryer to 170°C/340°F.
2. Place the apple chunks, blueberries, lemon juice and zest, half of the butter, half of the brown sugar, and cinnamon in a greased baking dish.
3. Combine thoroughly until all is well mixed.
4. Combine the flour with the remaining butter and brown sugar in a separate bowl. Stir until it forms a crumbly consistency.
5. Spread the crumb mixture over the fruit.
6. Bake in the air fryer for 10-15 minutes until golden and bubbling.
7. Serve and enjoy!

Variations & Ingredients Tips:

- Use other fruit like peaches, raspberries or rhubarb.
- Add rolled oats or nuts to the crumb topping.
- Serve with vanilla ice cream or custard.

Per Serving: Calories: 483; Total Fat: 20g; Saturated Fat: 12g; Sodium: 193mg; Total Carbohydrates: 77g; Dietary Fiber: 5g; Total Sugars: 52g; Protein: 3g

Coconut Rice Cake

Servings: 8 | Prep Time: 10 Minutes |

Cooking Time: 30 Minutes

Ingredients:

- 1 cup all-natural coconut water
- 1 cup unsweetened coconut milk
- 1 teaspoon almond extract
- ¼ teaspoon salt
- 4 tablespoons honey
- cooking spray
- ¾ cup raw jasmine rice
- 2 cups sliced or cubed fruit

Directions:

1. In a medium bowl, mix together the coconut water, coconut milk, almond extract, salt, and honey.
2. Spray air fryer baking pan with cooking spray and add the rice.
3. Pour liquid mixture over rice.
4. Cook at 180°C/360°F for 15 minutes. Stir and cook for 15 minutes longer or until rice grains are tender.
5. Allow cake to cool slightly. Run a dull knife around edge of cake, inside the pan. Turn the cake out onto a platter and garnish with fruit.

Variations & Ingredients Tips:

- Use brown rice, black rice, or wild rice for a nuttier flavor and chewier texture.
- Add shredded coconut to the batter for extra coconut goodness.
- Drizzle with coconut syrup or condensed milk before serving.

Per Serving: Calories: 200; Total Fat: 5g; Saturated Fat: 4g; Sodium: 100mg; Total Carbohydrates: 36g; Dietary Fiber: 1g; Total Sugars: 15g; Protein: 2g

Cherry Hand Pies

Servings: 8 | Prep Time: 20 Minutes | Cooking Time: 8 Minutes

Ingredients:

- 4 cups frozen or canned pitted tart
- cherries (if using canned, drain and

pat dry)
- 2 teaspoons lemon juice
- 1/2 cup sugar
- 1/4 cup cornstarch
- 1 teaspoon vanilla

extract
- 1 Basic Pie Dough (see the preceding recipe) or store-bought pie dough

Directions:

1. In a saucepan, cook cherries and lemon juice over medium heat for 10 minutes until cherries break down.
2. Mix sugar and cornstarch, then stir into cherries. Cook 2-3 minutes until thickened.
3. Remove from heat, stir in vanilla and let cool to room temp (30 mins).
4. Divide pie dough into 8 pieces. Roll each into a circle 0.5-cm thick.
5. Place 1/4 cup filling in the center of each circle. Fold into a half-circle and crimp edges with a fork to seal. Prick tops.
6. Preheat air fryer to 175°C/350°F.
7. Place pies in single layer in air fryer basket and spray with cooking spray.
8. Cook for 8-10 minutes until golden brown.

Variations & Ingredients Tips:

- Use other fruit fillings like apple, blueberry or peach.
- Brush tops with egg wash before baking for a shiny finish.
- Dust with powdered sugar or drizzle with glaze after baking.

Per Serving: Calories: 267; Total Fat: 9g; Saturated Fat: 3g; Sodium: 116mg; Total Carbohydrates: 44g; Dietary Fiber: 2g; Total Sugars: 22g; Protein: 3g

Mini Carrot Cakes

Servings: 6 | Prep Time: 15 Minutes | Cooking Time: 25 Minutes

Ingredients:

- 1 cup grated carrots
- 1/4 cup raw honey

- 1/4 cup olive oil
- 1/2 tsp vanilla ex-

tract
- 1/2 tsp lemon zest
- 1 egg
- 1/4 cup applesauce
- 1 1/3 cups flour
- 3/4 tsp baking powder
- 1/2 tsp baking soda
- 1/2 tsp ground cinnamon

- 1/4 tsp ground nutmeg
- 1/8 tsp ground ginger
- 1/8 tsp salt
- 1/4 cup chopped hazelnuts
- 2 tbsp chopped sultanas

Directions:

1. Preheat air fryer to 190°C/380°F.
2. Mix carrots, honey, oil, vanilla, zest, egg and applesauce.
3. In another bowl, sift flour, baking powder, soda, spices and salt.
4. Add dry to wet ingredients and mix just until combined.
5. Fold in hazelnuts and sultanas.
6. Fill greased muffin cups 3/4 full with batter.
7. Place cups in air fryer basket and bake 10-12 mins until a toothpick comes out clean.
8. Serve and enjoy!

Variations & Ingredients Tips:

- Use maple syrup or agave instead of honey.
- Add raisins, walnuts or shredded coconut.
- Top with cream cheese frosting.

Per Serving (2 mini cakes): Calories: 312; Total Fat: 13g; Saturated Fat: 2g; Sodium: 256mg; Total Carbohydrates: 46g; Dietary Fiber: 4g; Total Sugars: 19g; Protein: 5g

Strawberry Donuts

Servings: 4 | Prep Time: 25 Minutes | Cooking Time: 55 Minutes

Ingredients:

- 3/4 cup Greek yogurt
- 2 tbsp maple syrup
- 1 tbsp vanilla extract
- 2 tsp active dry

yeast
- 1 1/2 cups all-purpose flour
- 3 tbsp milk
- 1/2 cup strawberry jam

Directions:

1. Preheat air fryer to 175°C/350°F.
2. Whisk the Greek yogurt, maple syrup, vanilla extract, and yeast until well combined. Then toss in flour until you get a sticky dough.
3. Let rest covered for 10 minutes. Flour a parchment paper on a flat surface, lay the dough, sprinkle with some flour, and flatten to 1.3cm thick with a rolling pin.
4. Using a 8cm cookie cutter, cut the donuts. Repeat the process until no dough is left.
5. Place the donuts in the basket and let rise for 15-20 minutes. Spread some milk on top of each donut and Air Fry for 4 minutes. Turn the donuts, spread more milk, and Air Fry for 4 more minutes until golden brown.
6. Let cool for 15 minutes. Using a knife, cut the donuts 3/4 lengthwise, brush 1 tbsp of strawberry jam on each and close them. Serve.

Variations & Ingredients Tips:

● Use other jam flavors like blueberry or raspberry.
● Coat in cinnamon-sugar after baking.
● Fill with cream cheese frosting.

Per Serving: Calories: 320; Total Fat: 3g; Saturated Fat: 1g; Cholesterol: 5mg; Sodium: 100mg; Total Carbs: 62g; Dietary Fiber: 2g; Total Sugars: 20g; Protein: 8g

Raspberry Empanada

Servings: 6 | Prep Time: 15 Minutes | Cooking Time: 35 Minutes

Ingredients:

● 1 can raspberry pie filling
● 1 puff pastry dough
● 1 egg white, beaten

Directions:

1. Preheat air fryer to 190°C/370°F.
2. Unroll the two sheets of dough and cut into 4 squares each, or 8 squares total.
3. Scoop 1/2 to 1 tbsp of the raspberry pie filling in the center of each square.

4. Brush the edges with egg white. Fold diagonally to form a triangle and close the turnover. Press the edges with the back of a fork to seal.
5. Arrange the turnovers in a single layer in the greased basket. Spray the empanadas with cooking oil and Bake for 8 minutes.
6. Let them sit in the air fryer for 3-4 minutes to cool before removing. Repeat for the other batch. Serve and enjoy!

Variations & Ingredients Tips:

● Use other pie fillings like apple, cherry or lemon.
● Dust with powdered sugar or cinnamon sugar before serving.
● Brush the tops with egg wash for a shiny finish.

Per Serving: Calories: 225; Total Fat: 11g; Saturated Fat: 4g; Cholesterol: 15mg; Sodium: 135mg; Total Carbs: 30g; Dietary Fiber: 1g; Total Sugars: 13g; Protein: 3g

Bananas Foster Bread Pudding

Servings: 4 | Prep Time: 15 Minutes | Cooking Time: 25 Minutes

Ingredients:

● 1/2 cup brown sugar
● 3 eggs
● 3/4 cup half and half
● 1 teaspoon pure vanilla extract
● 6 cups cubed Kings
● Hawaiian bread (1.3-cm cubes), 220-g
● 2 bananas, sliced
● 1 cup caramel sauce, plus more for serving

Directions:

1. Preheat the air fryer to 175°C/350°F.
2. Combine the brown sugar, eggs, half and half and vanilla in a bowl, whisk until smooth.
3. Stir in the cubed bread and toss to coat. Let sit for 10 minutes to absorb liquid.
4. Mix the sliced bananas and caramel sauce together in a separate bowl.

5. Fill 4 greased 220-g ramekins with half the bread cubes. Top with caramel-banana mixture and remaining bread.
6. Cover ramekins with tented foil.
7. Air fry two at a time for 25 minutes.
8. Let cool slightly and serve warm with extra caramel sauce and ice cream if desired.

Variations & Ingredients Tips:

● Use challah or brioche bread instead of Hawaiian.
● Add chopped pecans or walnuts to the bread pudding.
● Substitute rum for vanilla extract.

Per Serving: Calories: 543; Total Fat: 16g; Saturated Fat: 6g; Sodium: 415mg; Total Carbohydrates: 92g; Dietary Fiber: 3g; Total Sugars: 56g; Protein: 11g

Fried Banana S'mores

Servings: 4 | Prep Time: 10 Minutes | Cooking Time: 6 Minutes

Ingredients:

- 4 bananas
- 3 tablespoons mini semi-sweet chocolate chips
- 3 tablespoons mini
- peanut butter chips
- 3 tablespoons mini marshmallows
- 3 tablespoons graham cracker cereal

Directions:

1. Preheat the air fryer to 200°C/400°F.
2. Slice into the un-peeled bananas lengthwise along the inside of the curve, but do not slice through the bottom of the peel. Open the banana slightly to form a pocket.
3. Fill each pocket with chocolate chips, peanut butter chips and marshmallows. Poke the graham cracker cereal into the filling.
4. Place the bananas in the air fryer basket, resting them on the side of the basket and each other to keep them upright with the filling facing up. Air-fry for 6 minutes, or until the bananas are soft to the touch, the peels have blackened and

the chocolate and marshmallows have melted and toasted.
5. Let them cool for a couple of minutes and then simply serve with a spoon to scoop out the filling.

Variations & Ingredients Tips:

● Use Nutella or cookie butter instead of peanut butter chips.
● Add a sprinkle of shredded coconut or chopped nuts to the filling.
● Serve with a scoop of vanilla or banana ice cream.

Per Serving: Calories: 270; Total Fat: 8g; Saturated Fat: 4.5g; Sodium: 50mg; Total Carbohydrates: 51g; Dietary Fiber: 5g; Total Sugars: 32g; Protein: 4g

Pear And Almond Biscotti Crumble

Servings: 6 | Prep Time: 15 Minutes | Cooking Time: 65 Minutes

Ingredients:

- 18-cm cake pan or ceramic dish
- 3 pears, peeled, cored and sliced
- 1/2 cup brown sugar
- 1/4 teaspoon ground ginger
- 1 teaspoon ground cinnamon
- 1/8 teaspoon ground nutmeg
- 2 tablespoons cornstarch
- 1 1/4 cups (4 to 5) almond biscotti, coarsely crushed
- 1/4 cup all-purpose flour
- 1/4 cup sliced almonds
- 1/4 cup butter, melted

Directions:

1. Combine the pears, brown sugar, ginger, cinnamon, nutmeg and cornstarch in a bowl. Toss to combine and then pour the pear mixture into a greased 18-cm cake pan or ceramic dish.
2. Combine the crushed biscotti, flour, almonds and melted butter in a medium bowl. Toss with

a fork until the mixture resembles large crumbles. Sprinkle the biscotti crumble over the pears and cover the pan with aluminum foil.

3. Preheat the air fryer to 175°C/350°F.
4. Air-fry at 175°C/350°F for 60 minutes. Remove the aluminum foil and air-fry for an additional 5 minutes to brown the crumble layer.
5. Serve warm.

Variations & Ingredients Tips:

- Use apples or a mix of pears and apples for the fruit base.
- Substitute brown sugar with maple syrup or honey.
- Add spices like cardamom or star anise to the crumble topping.

Per Serving: Calories: 340; Total Fat: 15g; Saturated Fat: 5g; Cholesterol: 20mg; Sodium: 125mg; Total Carbs: 50g; Dietary Fiber: 5g; Total Sugars: 28g; Protein: 5g

Banana Bread Cake

Servings: 6 | Prep Time: 15 Minutes | Cooking Time: 18-22 Minutes

Ingredients:

- 3/4 cup plus 2 tablespoons All-purpose flour
- 1/2 teaspoon Baking powder
- 1/4 teaspoon Baking soda
- 1/4 teaspoon Table salt
- 4 tablespoons (1/4 cup/1/2 stick) Butter, at room temperature
- 1/2 cup Granulated white sugar
- 2 Small ripe bananas, peeled
- 5 tablespoons Pasteurized egg substitute, such as Egg Beaters
- 1/4 cup Buttermilk
- 3/4 teaspoon Vanilla extract
- Baking spray

Directions:

1. Preheat the air fryer to 165°C/325°F (or 170°C/330°F, if that's the closest setting).
2. Mix the flour, baking powder, baking soda, and salt in a small bowl until well combined.
3. Using an electric hand mixer at medium speed, beat the butter and sugar in a medium bowl until creamy and smooth, about 3 minutes.
4. Beat in the bananas until smooth. Then beat in egg substitute, buttermilk, and vanilla until uniform.
5. Add the flour mixture and beat at low speed until smooth and creamy.
6. Use baking spray to coat the inside of a 15cm, 18cm or 20cm round cake pan. Spread batter into the pan.
7. Set the pan in the basket and air-fry for 18 mins for 15cm, 20 mins for 18cm, or 22 mins for 20cm pan.
8. Check at 16 mins, cake is done when browned and set in center.
9. Let cool 10 mins before unmolding. Cool completely before slicing into wedges.

Variations & Ingredients Tips:

- Add chopped nuts or chocolate chips to the batter.
- Use mashed sweet potatoes or pumpkin instead of bananas.
- Top with cream cheese frosting.

Per Serving: Calories: 256; Total Fat: 10g; Saturated Fat: 6g; Sodium: 290mg; Total Carbohydrates: 37g; Dietary Fiber: 1g; Total Sugars: 18g; Protein: 4g

Ricotta Stuffed Apples

Servings: 4 | Prep Time: 10 Minutes | Cooking Time: 25 Minutes

Ingredients:

- 1/2 cup cheddar cheese
- 1/4 cup raisins
- 2 apples
- 1/2 tsp ground cinnamon

Directions:

1. Preheat air fryer to 175°C/350°F.
2. Combine cheddar cheese and raisins in a bowl and set aside.

3. Chop apples lengthwise and discard the core and stem.
4. Sprinkle each half with cinnamon and stuff each half with 1/4 of the cheddar mixture.
5. Bake for 7 minutes, turn, and Bake for 13 minutes more until the apples are soft.
6. Serve immediately.

Variations & Ingredients Tips:

● Use a mix of cheddar and cream cheese for the stuffing.
● Add chopped nuts like walnuts or pecans to the stuffing.
● Drizzle with honey before serving.

Per Serving: Calories: 180; Total Fat: 9g; Saturated Fat: 5g; Cholesterol: 25mg; Sodium: 190mg; Total Carbs: 20g; Dietary Fiber: 3g; Total Sugars: 15g; Protein: 6g

Party S'mores

Servings: 6 | Prep Time: 5 Minutes | Cooking Time: 15 Minutes

Ingredients:

● 2 dark chocolate bars, cut into 12 pieces
● 12 buttermilk biscuits
● 12 marshmallows

Directions:

1. Preheat air fryer to 175°C/350°F.
2. Place 6 biscuits in the air fryer. Top each square with a piece of dark chocolate.
3. Bake for 2 minutes. Add a marshmallow to each piece of chocolate.
4. Cook for another minute. Remove and top with another piece of biscuit.
5. Serve warm.

Variations & Ingredients Tips:

● Use graham crackers instead of buttermilk biscuits for a more traditional s'more.
● Substitute dark chocolate with milk chocolate or white chocolate.
● Add a sprinkle of cinnamon or sea salt on top

for extra flavor.

Per Serving (2 s'mores): Calories: 280; Total Fat: 12g; Saturated Fat: 6g; Cholesterol: 5mg; Sodium: 370mg; Total Carbs: 40g; Dietary Fiber: 1g; Total Sugars: 18g; Protein: 4g

White Chocolate Cranberry Blondies

Servings: 6 | Prep Time: 10 Minutes | Cooking Time: 18 Minutes

Ingredients:

● 1/3 cup butter
● 1/2 cup sugar
● 1 teaspoon vanilla extract
● 1 large egg
● 1 cup all-purpose flour
● 1/2 teaspoon baking powder
● 1/8 teaspoon salt
● 1/4 cup dried cranberries
● 1/4 cup white chocolate chips

Directions:

1. Preheat the air fryer to 160°C/320°F.
2. In a large bowl, cream the butter with the sugar and vanilla extract. Whisk in the egg and set aside.
3. In a separate bowl, mix the flour with the baking powder and salt. Then gently mix the dry ingredients into the wet. Fold in the cranberries and chocolate chips.
4. Liberally spray an oven-safe 18cm springform pan with olive oil and pour the batter into the pan.
5. Cook for 17 minutes or until a toothpick inserted in the center comes out clean.
6. Remove and let cool 5 minutes before serving.

Variations & Ingredients Tips:

● Use dried tart cherries instead of cranberries.
● Add chopped nuts like pecans or walnuts.
● Drizzle with a vanilla glaze after baking.

Per Serving: Calories: 360; Total Fat: 17g; Saturated Fat: 10g; Cholesterol: 60mg; Sodium: 125mg; Total Carbs: 48g; Dietary Fiber: 1g; Total

Sugars: 27g; Protein: 4g

Mixed Berry Pie

Servings: 4 | Prep Time: 15 Minutes | Cooking Time: 25 Minutes

Ingredients:

- 2/3 cup blackberries, cut into thirds
- 1/4 cup sugar
- 2 tbsp cornstarch
- 1/4 tsp vanilla extract
- 1/4 tsp peppermint extract
- 1/2 tsp lemon zest
- 1 cup sliced strawberries
- 1 cup raspberries
- 1 refrigerated pie-crust
- 1 large egg

Directions:

1. Mix sugar, cornstarch, vanilla, peppermint and zest in a bowl.
2. Gently toss in all berries until coated. Pour into a greased baking dish.
3. On a surface, roll out dough into a 18-cm round. Cover dish with dough and crimp edges.
4. Cut 4 slits in the top to vent. Brush with beaten egg.
5. Preheat air fryer to 175°C/350°F.
6. Air fry for 15 mins until crust is golden and berries are bubbling.
7. Let cool 15 mins before serving warm.

Variations & Ingredients Tips:

- Use a graham cracker or cookie crust instead of pie dough.
- Add a crumble or streusel topping before baking.
- Serve with vanilla ice cream or whipped cream.

Per Serving: Calories: 244; Total Fat: 7g; Saturated Fat: 2g; Sodium: 145mg; Total Carbohydrates: 43g; Dietary Fiber: 5g; Total Sugars: 24g; Protein: 4g

Peanut Butter Cup Doughnut Holes

Servings: 24 | Prep Time: 30 Minutes (plus Rising Time) | Cooking Time: 4 Minutes

Ingredients:

- 1 1/2 cups bread flour
- 1 teaspoon active dry yeast
- 1 tablespoon sugar
- 1/4 teaspoon salt
- 1/2 cup warm milk
- 1/2 teaspoon vanilla extract
- 2 egg yolks
- 2 tablespoons melted butter
- 24 miniature peanut butter cups, plus a few more for garnish
- Vegetable oil, in a spray bottle
- Doughnut Topping:
- 1 cup chocolate chips
- 2 tablespoons milk

Directions:

1. Combine the flour, yeast, sugar and salt in a bowl. Add the milk, vanilla, egg yolks and butter. Mix well until the dough starts to come together. Transfer the dough to a floured surface and knead by hand for 2 minutes. Shape the dough into a ball and transfer it to a large oiled bowl. Cover the bowl with a towel and let the dough rise in a warm place for 1 to 1 1/2 hours, until the dough has doubled in size.
2. When the dough has risen, punch it down and roll it into a 60-cm long log. Cut the dough into 24 pieces. Push a peanut butter cup into the center of each piece of dough, pinch the dough shut and roll it into a ball. Place the dough balls on a cookie sheet and let them rise in a warm place for 30 minutes.
3. Preheat the air fryer to 200°C/400°F.
4. Spray or brush the dough balls lightly with vegetable oil. Air-fry eight at a time, at 200°C/400°F for 4 minutes, turning them over halfway through the cooking process.
5. While the doughnuts are air frying, prepare the topping. Place the chocolate chips and milk in a microwave safe bowl. Microwave on high for 1 minute. Stir and microwave for an additional 30 seconds if necessary to get all the chips to melt.

Stir until the chips are melted and smooth.

6. Dip the top half of the doughnut holes into the melted chocolate. Place them on a rack to set up for just a few minutes and watch them disappear.

Variations & Ingredients Tips:

● Use different flavors of mini cups like white chocolate, dark chocolate or caramel.
● Roll doughnuts in cinnamon sugar instead of dipping in chocolate.
● Make a peanut butter glaze by mixing powdered sugar, peanut butter and a little milk.

Per Serving (1 doughnut hole): Calories: 120; Total Fat: 6g; Saturated Fat: 3g; Cholesterol: 20mg; Sodium: 60mg; Total Carbs: 14g; Dietary Fiber: 1g; Total Sugars: 6g; Protein: 3g

Midnight Nutella® Banana Sandwich

Servings: 2 | Prep Time: 5 Minutes | Cooking Time: 8 Minutes

Ingredients:

● Butter, softened
● 4 slices white bread*
● 1/4 cup chocolate

hazelnut spread (Nutella®)
● 1 banana

Directions:

1. Preheat air fryer to 190°C/370°F.
2. Butter one side of all bread slices.
3. Flip over and spread Nutella on the other sides.
4. Slice banana and place pieces on 2 bread slices. Top with remaining bread, buttered side up.
5. Cut sandwiches in half and place in air fryer basket.
6. Air fry for 5 minutes, then flip and cook 2-3 more minutes until browned.
7. Let cool slightly before serving.

Variations & Ingredients Tips:

● Use different nut butters like almond or cashew.

● Add sliced strawberries or marshmallow fluff.
● Use brioche, challah or other soft bread.

Per Serving (1 sandwich): Calories: 453; Total Fat: 21g; Saturated Fat: 7g; Sodium: 375mg; Total Carbohydrates: 59g; Dietary Fiber: 4g; Total Sugars: 24g; Protein: 9g

Lemon Iced Donut Balls

Servings: 6 | Prep Time: 10 Minutes | Cooking Time: 25 Minutes

Ingredients:

● 1 can jumbo biscuit dough
● 2 tsp lemon juice
● 1/2 cup icing sugar, sifted

Directions:

1. Preheat air fryer to 180°C/360°F.
2. Divide biscuit dough into 16 equal portions and roll into 3.8-cm balls.
3. Place balls in greased air fryer basket.
4. Air fry for 8 minutes, flipping once halfway.
5. In a bowl, mix icing sugar and lemon juice until smooth.
6. Spread icing over warm donut balls.
7. Let icing set slightly before serving.

Variations & Ingredients Tips:

● Add lemon or orange zest to the icing.
● Roll donut balls in cinnamon-sugar before baking.
● Make a glaze icing by adding milk instead of lemon juice.

Per Serving (3 donut balls): Calories: 211; Total Fat: 5g; Saturated Fat: 2g; Sodium: 282mg; Total Carbohydrates: 39g; Dietary Fiber: 0g; Total Sugars: 14g; Protein: 3g

Cinnamon Sugar Banana Rolls

Servings: 6 | Prep Time: 15 Minutes | Cooking Time: 8 Minutes

Ingredients:

- 1/4 cup Granulated white sugar
- 2 teaspoons Ground cinnamon
- 2 tablespoons Peach or apricot jam or orange marmalade
- 6 Spring roll wrappers, thawed if necessary
- 2 Ripe bananas, peeled and cut into 8-cm sections
- 1 Large egg, well beaten
- Vegetable oil spray

Directions:

1. Preheat the air fryer to 200°C/400°F.
2. Mix sugar and cinnamon in a bowl. Loosen jam/marmalade with a fork.
3. Place banana section at edge of spring roll wrapper. Top with 1 tsp jam.
4. Roll banana in wrapper, folding sides over first, then rolling up sealing with egg wash.
5. Repeat with remaining rolls.
6. Mist rolls with oil spray.
7. Air fry for 8 minutes until crisp and golden.
8. Transfer to a wire rack and cool 5-30 minutes before serving.

Variations & Ingredients Tips:

- Use other fruit besides banana like apple or pear slices.
- Sprinkle with powdered sugar after cooking.
- Serve with caramel or chocolate sauce for dipping.

Per Serving: Calories: 150; Total Fat: 2g; Saturated Fat: 0g; Sodium: 95mg; Total Carbohydrates: 32g; Dietary Fiber: 2g; Total Sugars: 16g; Protein: 3g

Chocolate Cake

Servings: 8 | Prep Time: 10 Minutes |

Cooking Time: 20 Minutes

Ingredients:

- 1/2 cup sugar
- 1/4 cup flour, plus 3 tablespoons
- 3 tablespoons cocoa
- 1/2 teaspoon baking powder
- 1/2 teaspoon baking soda
- 1/4 teaspoon salt
- 1 egg
- 2 tablespoons oil
- 1/2 cup milk
- 1/2 teaspoon vanilla extract

Directions:

1. Preheat air fryer to 165°C/330°F.
2. Grease and flour a 15x15cm baking pan.
3. In a bowl, stir together sugar, flours, cocoa, baking powder, soda and salt.
4. Add egg, oil, milk and vanilla. Beat with a whisk until smooth.
5. Pour batter into prepared pan.
6. Bake at 330°F for 20 minutes until toothpick inserted comes out clean.

Variations & Ingredients Tips:

- Add chocolate chips or chopped nuts to the batter.
- Substitute buttermilk for a moister cake.
- Top with chocolate frosting or powdered sugar.

Per Serving: Calories: 149; Total Fat: 4g; Saturated Fat: 1g; Sodium: 158mg; Total Carbohydrates: 26g; Dietary Fiber: 1g; Total Sugars: 14g; Protein: 3g

INDEX

Printed in Great Britain
by Amazon

53228907R00057